AF253263

THE
WEDDING
PHOTOGRAPHY

LETTERS

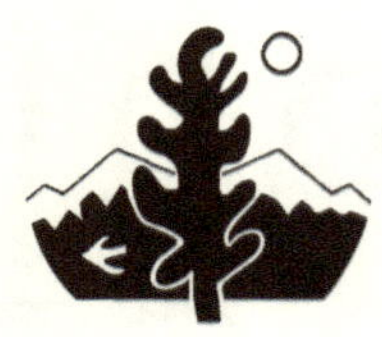

The Wedding Photography Letters by Brad Wood

Published by The Woods Photography 2022

www.thewoodsphotography.nz

Copyright © 2022 Brad Wood

Cover and illustrations by Petra Oomen

ISBN (Paperback): 978-0-473-64293-8

ISBN (Hardback): 978-0-473-64294-5

ISBN (Kindle): 978-0-473-64295-2

THE WEDDING PHOTOGRAPHY

LETTERS

WORDS TO ENCOURAGE, EQUIP, AND INSPIRE CREATIVE WEDDING PHOTOGRAPHERS

WRITTEN BY
BRAD WOOD

ILLUSTRATED BY
PETRA OOMEN

FOR THEO

THANK YOU FOR OUR CONVERSATIONS AND FRIENDSHIP, WHICH
INSPIRED THIS BOOK.

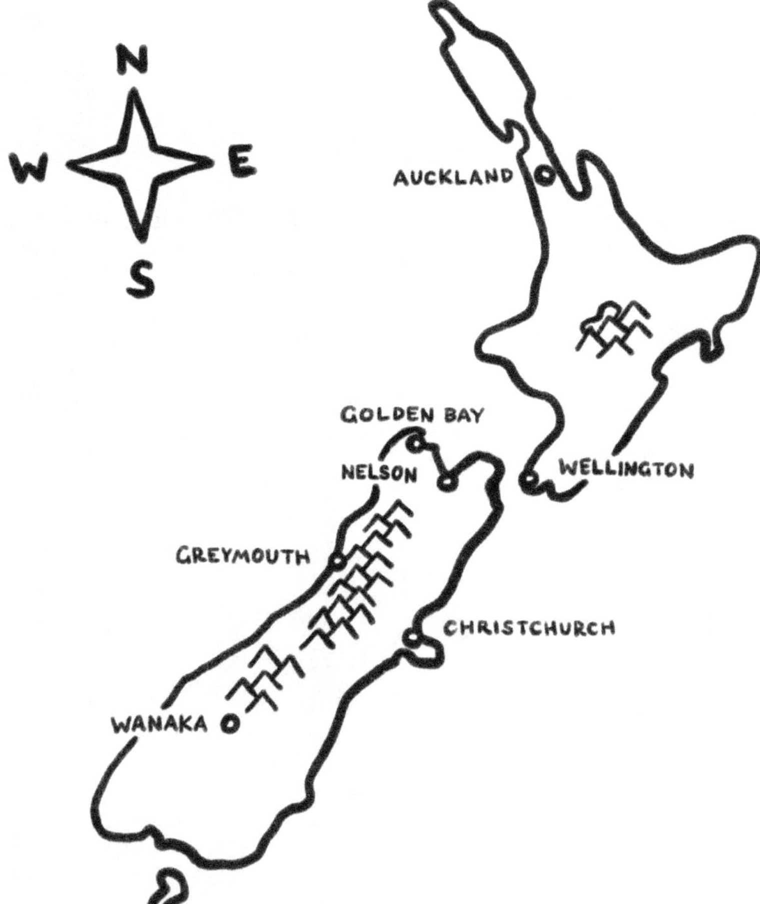

N
W
E
S
AUCKLAND
GOLDEN BAY
NELSON
WELLINGTON
GREYMOUTH
CHRISTCHURCH
WANAKA

CONTENTS

PART 1
WORKING
ON
YOURSELF

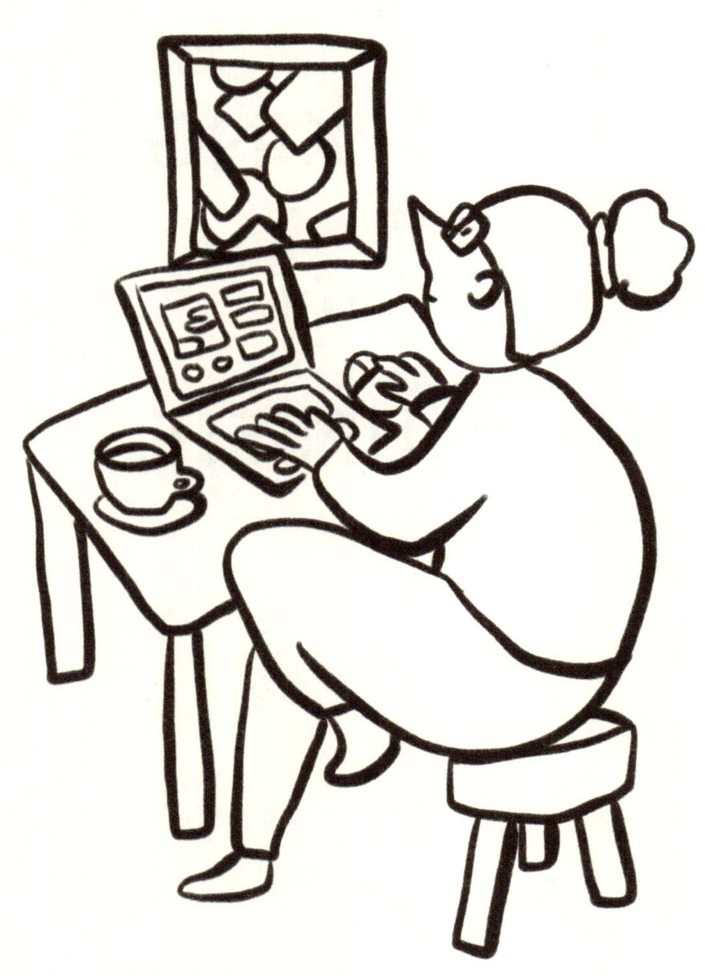

1 GETTING INSPIRED

IN PHOTOGRAPHY, THE SMALLEST THING CAN BE A GREAT SUBJECT

HENRI CARTIER-BRESSON

Dear Charlie,

Inspiration is an unruly map within your mind, alive and ever-changing. It will lead you to unexpected and foreign places. There's no way of knowing whether it will guide you to success or failure, but what I do know is this: inspiration is vital to the creative life. What inspires you? What drives you to create? I'll admit that I'm addicted to beautiful books. They can be art books, classic novels, graphic novels, or the illustrated Harry Potter. It doesn't really matter. If it's beautiful and visual, it draws me in — it inspires me.

Often, you can find me looking for beautiful second-hand book bargains — a literary version of a metal detector. My personal creative diet tends to consist of printed photographs and written words.

In 2018, I was hunting online for some illustrated treasures and came across a book I had dreamed of owning. It was a copy of Henri Cartier-Bresson's masterpiece, *The Decisive Moment* —selling for $1.

I do a lot of second-hand book buying and this has to be the best deal I have ever come across. When I received the book, it quickly became the favourite in my collection. Printed beautifully, with inspirational words and incredible images. This was a book made for energising its viewers.

The inspirational work of artists you admire is the food that will sustain your creative journey. Without it, you'll run dry, so it's important to make sure you're feeding yourself well every day. In your previous letter, you mentioned a number of photographers you admire on social media. Keep being inspired by their work, but don't be afraid of trying something new. The beautiful thing about inspiration is that it often comes from unexpected places.

Henri Cartier-Bresson was born in 1908 in France and was a master of candid street photography. He was a founding member of Magnum — one of the world's great photography agencies — and has inspired millions of photographers. When I hold his book, the images seem to pierce my soul and spark creative visions. This is what inspiration means to me — being moved to create by the work of others. You need inspiration as an artist. It is the fuel that will ignite the engine of your creativity. Without it, you will be a photographer with technical camera knowledge, but will never create any work of note.

Much like how the physical food we eat has a direct impact on the health of our bodies, our creative diet impacts the work we create. The books you read, the social media accounts you follow, the movies you watch and the photographers you look up to - these things will have a direct affect on the work you create, they impact our formation as people.

I particularly enjoy red liquorice filled with sour sherbet. It tastes amazing and delivers a direct hit of sucrose into the bloodstream. Could I eat one piece every day? Definitely. Could I eat it for a main meal? Definitely not.

Social media, as inspiration, is like candy. It tastes great and gives a quick hit, but is not suitable for a long-term creative diet. Creative work fuelled by social media will starve your photography from the vital nutrients it needs to develop.

The best way to up your inspirational intake is to find excellent sources of physical inspiration. Head to your local library and check out some art books. Take a walk to an art gallery and enjoy looking at creative works of art. It doesn't have to be photography or even related to photography to be worthwhile.

Inspiration can come from any artistic expression.

Don't feel you only need to be looking at the medium you've chosen to create with. Art has only been digital since 1980. It has been physical since 10,000 BC. Most art was created to be experienced without a screen, so go get physical.

Not all digital art is bad — far from it! But if you want to get the most out of art viewed through a screen, then you need to be intentional. Scrolling on a mobile device is not great for experiencing art. When you do this, great work gets missed or diluted by the sheer volume of content. It also diminishes the fine details of a work — you can only see so much with six inches of real estate.

Be intentional about how you are inspired on your device. A great way to do this is through watching documentaries and interviews with artists. Experiencing the creative process through the journey of others is a highly effective way to learn and be inspired. Often, these documentaries are free to access or relatively inexpensive.

You don't need to commit large amounts of time to inspiration. Ten minutes of intentional inspiration is hugely valuable and you can make time for it in many places. I used to hate doing the dishes and would avoid them at all costs. That was until I started watching interviews with artists or interesting people while I did them. Not only am I getting inspired, but it also makes my wife, Claudia, very happy.

It takes a while to build up a list of photographers and artists whose work you love. Since the start of my career, I've found some amazing artists who fuel my creativity. Most I will never have the chance to meet in person, but I am blessed that they gifted me their work through books, films, and prints.

As I go through the list, it's noticeable that none of my photographic heroes are wedding photographers. Artists outside of your genre can make a hugely positive impact on your work. I find my greatest sources of inspiration are often not photographers at all. Here are a few of my photographic heroes if you need a place to start your own list of artists who inspire you:

- Henri Cartier-Bresson

- Alex Webb

- Sally Mann

- Robert Capa

- Vivian Maier

- Elliot Erwitt

- Sebastião Salgado

- Ansel Adams

- Robert Frank

- Steve McCurry

- Dawoud Bey

Each of these artists has had a major impact on the way I see and create photographs. Not only through their works, but also through learning about their creative process — the method of how they go about making images.

This letter is all about making time to be intentional with your inspiration. This week, find an artist whose work inspires you, it could be a photographer or a painter or a poet. Once you've found that person, find an exhibition, book, or documentary that showcases their work.

Try to avoid finding their work through a hashtag on social media or looking at their website. Find something that will allow you to have a focused time where you can enjoy their creativity and learn their process.

Allow your mind the freedom to explore unexpected places. Dedicate time to view their art in a way that is free from distraction. Turn your phone off, even if it's for fifteen minutes. Trust me, it will be good for your health.

Your friend,

B.W.

2 TALENT & TASTE

IF YOUR PICTURES AREN'T GOOD ENOUGH, YOU AREN'T CLOSE ENOUGH

ROBERT CAPA

Dear Charlie,

Taste in photography is something that many people naturally have. You clearly have good taste. The photographers you follow are some of the best in the business. It's important to have excellent sources of inspiration, but I noticed your frustration in the previous letter. You had tried to imitate an image, but your vision didn't translate well to a photograph.

When a photographer looks at a picture, they know without thinking whether it is inspired or mundane. They know what makes a beautiful picture. Some photographers, inspired by the creative work of others, seek to create similar pictures. They feel the thrill of excitement in capturing a beautiful moment, only to have their dream stall after comparing their work with the source of inspiration. Sound familiar?

It's as if you've received a knockout punch within the first minute of round one. Before creating the image, you had absolute confidence, but you underestimated the opponent. Your taste was no match for your talent.

Talent in photography is something you have to fight for. Like a boxer contending, you step into the ring prepared to fight. Will I knock them out? Will I be knocked out? Will I land enough hits to win after a long, bloody battle? How many times will I lose before my first win? But if you're driven to win, it doesn't matter how long it takes because you want it. Your passion will drive you to train and improve your craft.

You're at the start of your photography career and there is a chasm between your taste and talent. Ira Glass, presenter of *This American Life*, calls it 'The Gap'. There is no greater time in your creative career when you will feel the challenge of bridging 'The Gap' than in this moment. Your taste has collided with your burgeoning talent. The clean-up of your pride and broken hopes can take a while, but 'The Gap' can be conquered. No matter how challenging it seems.

It takes passion and a dedication to creating work… a lot of work. If you keep creating, you will look back one day and see that all your hard work was the only way across. Even if, to begin with, your taste recoils at what you have made.

In 2010, I was sitting at a cafe in Wellington with my friend, sharing the dream of becoming a photographer. I had just completed a business degree and realised I no longer had any desire to work in the corporate world.

Since my teens, all I'd wanted was to be a successful businessman. I desired to climb corporate ladders and invest in hedge funds. But after studying commerce for three years, the desire left me like a weekend lover fleeing on Sunday morning. Photography filled the space left by my prior romance.

Looking back, it seems strange that I would want to pick up a camera. I never studied photography in high school. My parents only brought our family camera out when we went on holiday. Even then, it tended to stay hidden in our luggage. I had neither skill nor pedigree, yet here I was, wanting to be a photographer. In all honesty, there was neither talent nor taste within me. I was starting from absolute zero. But there was a passion and willingness to dedicate the time to learn.

After graduating from university, I moved back to my hometown of Greymouth: a little town on the West Coast of New Zealand. I was determined to learn photography, and the only local photographer I knew was a man named Stewart Nimmo.

During our first meeting, I pleaded my case for wanting to learn and asked Stewart to be my mentor. Miraculously, he accepted me as a haphazard apprentice in exchange for working in his store.

I'm indebted to Stew for his generosity and patience with me as I stumbled my way through learning his craft. He taught me much, including the importance of sharing the gifts of skill and experience with others. I find it amazing how patient he was with me as I muddled through learning how to shoot, frame pictures, and learn the language of photography. I spent two years learning from Stewart. Throughout this time, I learnt an important principle — when you first start creating, it's going to be bad, wrong, or both. When you're learning, you need to create as much work as you can, as fast as you can.

This is the only way to quickly bridge the gap between your taste and your talent. This sounds fine in principle, but for a photographer, creating poor work is a struggle. Inferior work hits against your pride like a stubbed toe on concrete. But the pain is temporary, and it has a purpose. It's a necessary step on the path to being a successful photographer. When you're starting the creative journey, it's OK to make work you're not fully satisfied with. Keep going. One day, you'll look back and find that all the pictures you took which didn't quite meet your standard were important steps.

I believe in you. You have the passion and drive needed to become a brilliant photographer. Pick up a camera and train your hands into creating works that live up to your taste. Be bold and ask for help from others who are further along the journey than you. They don't even need to be a physical person. There are countless talented photographers who have shared their work, skills, and stories. Make them your mentors. Fight the good fight of talent and, eventually, your taste will win a round.

Your friend,

B.W.

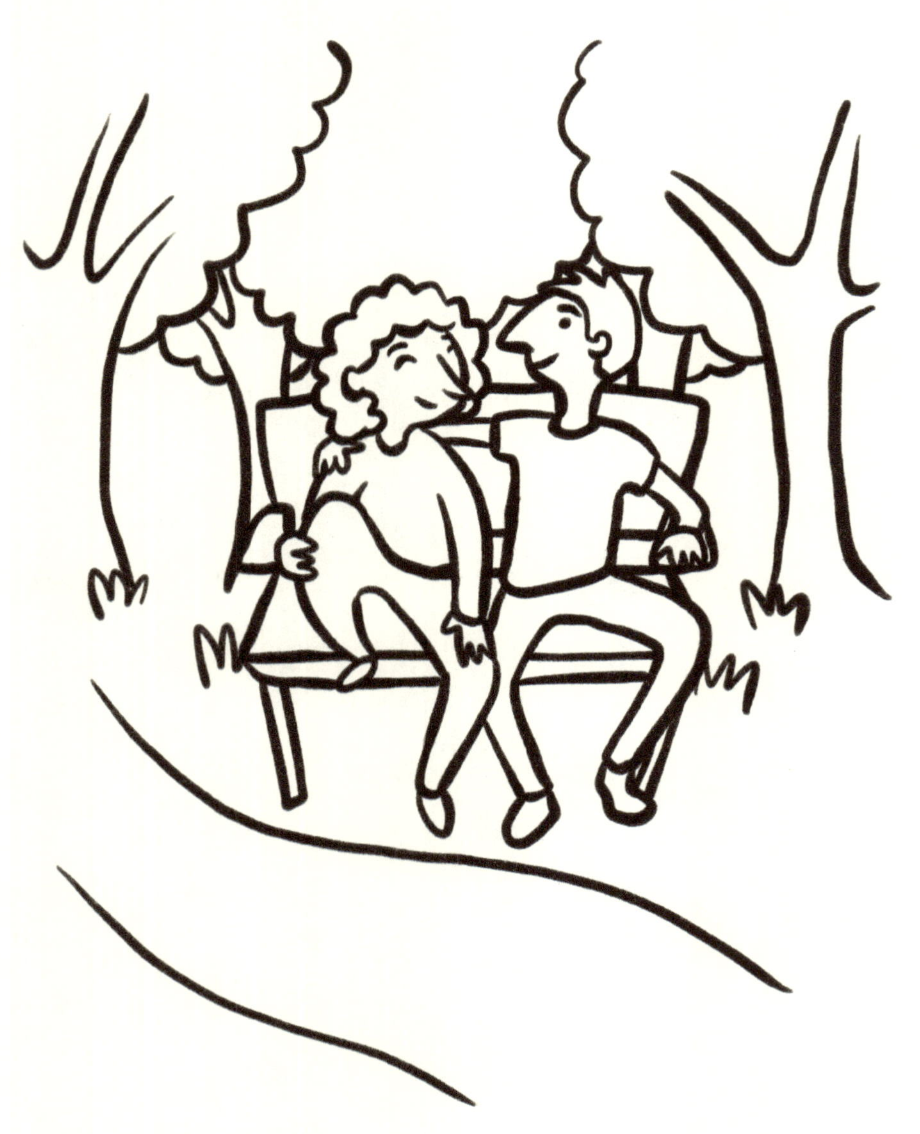

3 CONNECTION & COMMUNITY

THE GUY WHO TAKES A CHANCE, WHO WALKS THE LINE BETWEEN THE

KNOWN AND UNKNOWN, WHO IS UNAFRAID OF FAILURE, WILL SUCCEED

GORDON PARKS

Dear Charlie,

It was great to hear about your trip to the art gallery. It impressed me that you even brought a new friend with you. Art and romance have a long history together, so I'm sure that it went well. The further you go on this creative journey, the more you'll realise that sharing it with other like-minded people is vitally important. If there was a single piece of advice I could give you, it is this: build a strong network of supportive photographers.

In 2014, Claudia and I moved to Nelson — a small city at the top of the South Island of New Zealand. Two years prior, we started our photography business in Christchurch and things were going well. Our brand was growing, and we were getting increasing volumes of work. Things were looking great for our career —

until we moved towns.

At that time, we only had vague acquaintances in Nelson, and no close friends. So, we began building both our social network and business brand from scratch. The latter definitely seemed more difficult.

Before moving, we reached out to a local photographer who had featured our work in a magazine she edited. Aleisha was excited about our move and mentioned that if she ever had extra wedding inquiries, she would send them our way. In an industry that can be competitive, this was a very generous offer.

Our new friend ended up sending several weddings our way, which we booked. Without this connection, it would have taken a lot longer to build our brand in Nelson. In the creative arts, work creates more work. The more weddings you do, the better you will get and the more people will see and share your work. It's a matter of brand awareness. Every wedding you do means more potential clients seeing your images. As long as you are creating beautiful work, then it's going to lead to more bookings — unless you're a total dick, of course.

Years later, we were well established and had more work coming in than we could book. We received an email from a friend of ours who let us know about a photographer named Tim who was moving to Nelson. Our friend asked whether we had any work we were willing to pass on to him.

Tim's work was beautiful, and we were grateful to model the generosity we had received ourselves. After reaching out to him, we were able to pass on several weddings and it was fantastic to see him get established. It was such a blessing to help a new photographer get settled into Nelson. We also made a great friend who we continue to learn from and work on creative projects with.

Building new connections can sometimes result in rejection. But the payoff of growing relationships with other photographers is worth the risk. Without connections, you're going to cut yourself off from a beautiful part of this industry. Not only because of opportunities to share work, but because you'll go a lot further when you've got people cheering you on and giving support when things don't go to plan.

There are several ways in which you can develop connections, and they all require you to reach out and contact someone. There's no way around the fact that to build a connection, you're going to have to make the first move. You need to put yourself out there.

Send someone a direct message, invite a fellow photographer out for a coffee, or put on a craft beer tasting afternoon. It doesn't matter how you do it. Find a way that helps you build connections. This will be one of the most worthwhile investments you make in your career. You'll gain friends who help you become the best photographer you can be and help you when times get tough.

Recently, I received a notification from a wedding photography group I'm a part of, which read:

Anyone know what the deal is with the helicopter that went down in Christchurch? Is it one of our people? Get ready to get behind and support.

A few hours before this, a helicopter had crashed into a golf course carrying a bride, groom, and photographer. I didn't know the photographer, apart from some passing online interactions, but that didn't really matter. There is a tribal connection that develops between people who choose the same profession, which comes from a sense of shared vocation and experience.

It was amazing to see the outpouring of support as she began her journey of healing. There were words of encouragement, financial support, and practical help offered. It was a beautiful thing to see, and it came from her being connected to a community of like-minded people who share a profession. I've seen this happen several times. Photographers supporting others in tragedy, struggle, or helping someone settle into a new town. It doesn't matter whether they know each other well — that is the power of community.

The beauty of a healthy community is that it's not about individual members gaining selfish benefits. It's about each of the members helping one another. There are, of course, plenty of examples of people who never give back to communities they are a part of.

Sometimes you need to be careful or distance yourself from negative influences. But this is the exception, not the rule.

Being a part of a professional group where there is a culture of kindness and generosity is important. When you are, you'll be well equipped to face the challenges of wedding photography. So, get linked in with a community of your choice. There is likely to be a local group of photographers you can connect with. There will definitely be a national professional body to be a member of and there are thousands of online communities.

Remember that contribution is the heart of community. Be willing to help those who are helping you.

Connection and community are two sides of the same coin. We cannot separate one from the other. The more time you put into connecting with other photographers, the richer your sense of community will become. From connection and community come support, inspiration, friendship, learning, tools, and referrals. Time invested into building relationships is always worthwhile.

Here's a task to get you started. Jump onto social media and find a few local photographers you don't know. Send them a direct message or email and ask them out for a drink. Be honest with them about where you are at in your photography journey. Share with them that you would love to build connections with local photographers whose work inspires you.

If none of them get back to you, then try another three. You'll be amazed at what can come from these potential friendships.

Building a connection with someone you don't know is a risk. They might say no or even worse, they might say yes and then you have to make conversation for one hour with a stranger! But it's a risk worth taking — much like asking someone on a first date.

Your friend,

B.W.

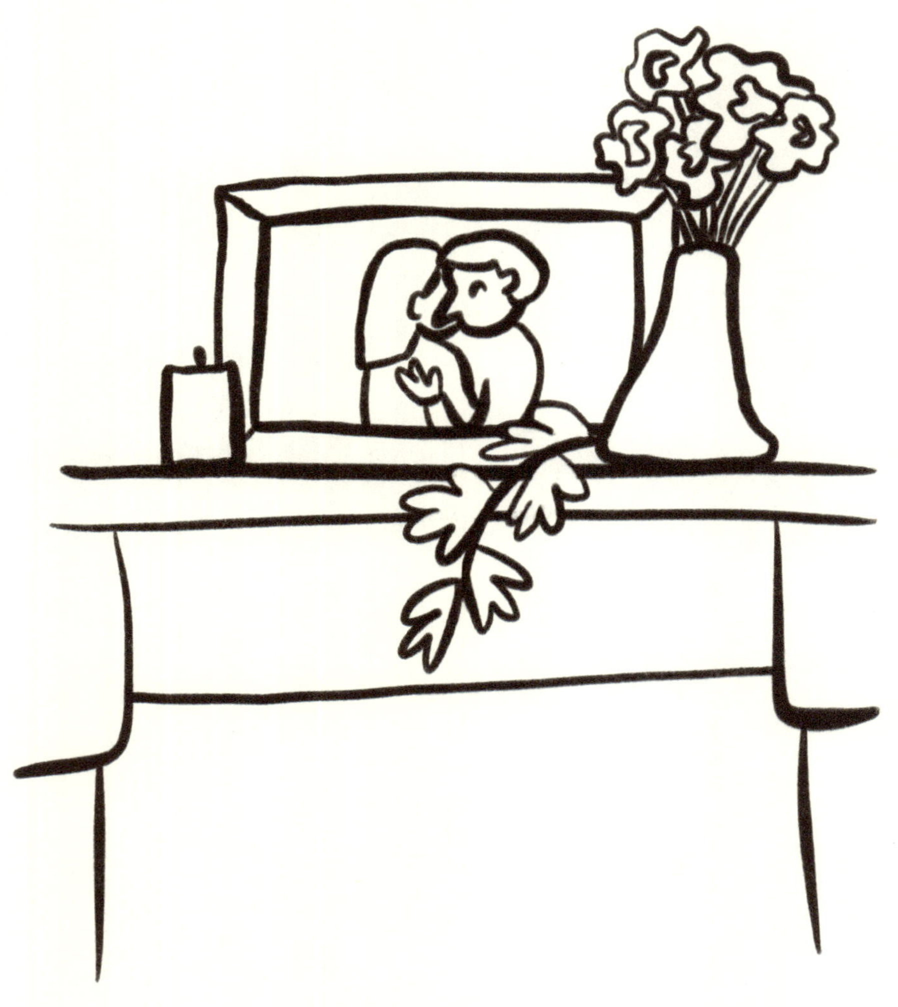

4 WHY PHOTOGRAPH A WEDDING?

UNLESS YOU PHOTOGRAPH WHAT YOU LOVE, YOU ARE NOT GOING

TO MAKE GOOD ART

SALLY MANN

Dear Charlie,

You're asking some great questions about wedding photography — that's what the purpose of these letters is, right? The answer is *yes,* but there is much more to this career than which camera to buy or how to pose a couple. Don't worry, we'll get to those things soon.

The first question we should ask is: *why photograph a wedding?* Then we can move on to the details. I want to start by helping you develop the mindset of an artist.

Ten years ago, I was photographing a winter wedding in Greymouth. The groom was standing at the altar, wearing what seemed to be a pirate costume — a thick red velvet cape, black shirt, and a white frilled cravat. His face had a look of relaxed excitement, expectant for what was to come. This was the day he had been waiting for.

The bride was one hour late to the ceremony, but he knew this was perfectly normal behaviour. When the bride arrived, she was wearing what looked like an elvish gown — a flowing polyester dress with tear-drop sleeves and an upside-down tiara upon her head.

Add to this torrential rain, gorse wine and possum pie, and you've got one of the most unique weddings I've ever experienced. But none of this mattered to the groom. He was about to marry the love of his life and I was about to photograph my first wedding.

Our industry is a strange combination of romance, beauty, and consumerism. As a photographer, you play the part of capturing one of the most important days of a person's life. At most weddings, more close friends and family are gathered in one place than at any other time in a person's life.

Even if you took out the momentous act of committing to another person for life, the gathering would still make for an incredibly important and memorable occasion.

Modern weddings vary wildly in price — some costing more than a university education, while others less than a modest second-hand car. But it doesn't really matter how much a couple spends on their wedding. What does matter is the couple and the people who they love.

For my friends on that wet winter afternoon, it was the happiest day of their life. For me, their wedding wasn't about capturing hero shots for social media or getting images printed in bridal magazines. It was about honouring the couple who were committing to each other for life. People who had chosen me to photograph their wedding.

It was about capturing their wedding day with passion and integrity. Was it my dream wedding? No, but it was theirs. And it was my job to capture it. On that day, I learnt a big lesson on why I photograph weddings. I photograph them because I believe in marriage. Weddings represent a beautiful binding of two unique people into one unique family. It's my belief in marriage, in all its complex beauty, that forms my *why*.

Wedding photography has to be one of the greatest jobs on Earth. We get paid to go to parties, travel to beautiful locations, and have incredible meals. What's not to like? But the perks of wedding photography will only drive you for so long. I would say two to three years before you get bored, and boredom as a creative person is not a fun thing.

I have been able to photograph weddings since 2012 because I believe in marriage. It's this *why* that has kept me motivated to continue capturing them for so long. It might take you a while to find a powerful reason why you want to be a wedding photographer, and that's OK. When you find your *why,* you will be a better photographer for it.

I'm going to lead you through a simple exercise to help you figure out why you want to photograph a wedding. Grab a pen and paper and set a six-minute timer on your phone.

In these six minutes, write all the reasons you want to photograph a wedding. Write whatever comes to your mind. There are no wrong reasons. Once your timer goes off, stop writing and set a two-minute timer. In these two minutes, choose your top five reasons, crossing off the ones that don't make the cut.

Finally, set a one-minute timer. Use this time to decide what your number one reason for photographing a wedding is. This should be the core reason you are choosing to step into this journey of photography.

There aren't any wrong reasons in this process. I'm sure your number one reason will change over time, but it's important to know what is driving you.

In 2015, I was in Blenheim photographing a wedding with Claudia. It was a warm spring day, and we were hunting for hero shots. We posed the couple at a local lookout with a backdrop of rolling hills touched by evening light. It was a beautiful shoot, and we captured some great photos for our portfolio. The couple loved them, but these weren't the ones they ended up treasuring.

The ones they valued most were a few simple photos of the bride and her father at their family home before the ceremony. There was one particular photo of them both in front of a bay window, looking at one another.

The light and composition weren't great. It was a simple moment of intimacy between two people who loved each other very much. A delicate moment. But at that point in my career, I definitely wouldn't have posted it on social media.

Two years after the wedding, the bride's father became sick with cancer and passed away. It was this photo that the bride shared on her Facebook page to honour his memory. She shared this photo, not because it was a hero shot but because it was a special moment that captured someone she held most dear.

It's photos like these which represent why I photograph weddings. There are other similar stories I could tell you, but I want you to create your own stories of capturing powerful memories — even if the wedding isn't quite your style.

Why do you want to photograph weddings?

Your friend,

B.W.

PART 2
CAPTURING
WEDDINGS

5 PREPARATION

IT IS A PRIVILEGE TO BE A PHOTOGRAPHER, TO HAVE THE

OPPORTUNITY TO BE THERE

SEBASTIÃO SALGADO

Dear Charlie,

It's exciting to hear you've booked another wedding, well done. I think you'll find as your work gets known and shared, a lot more work will come your way. It's a great feeling when an enquiry turns into a booking, particularly at the start of a career. But don't rest easy yet.

Once that contract has been signed, there's still work to be done before the wedding day. The last thing you want to do is turn up to a wedding unprepared.

Once, Claudia and I were booked to photograph a wedding in Hanmer Springs, a little alpine town in the South Island. It's one of our favourite places to relax, mostly because of the natural hot springs. The town has the distinct feeling of a miniature American ski resort. We travelled on Friday, allowing time to meet the couple, do location scouting, and have a swim in the pools before the wedding on Saturday.

We arrived and went straight to the venue so we could say hi to the couple. After a quick scout around, we bumped into the bride and groom, who were looking relaxed. We had a chat about the beautiful venue and perfect weather forecast. But when I mentioned looking forward to photographing their wedding tomorrow, a confused look came over their face. "Tomorrow? You mean Sunday, right?" they replied.

It took a moment to sink in. I had the day wrong! Earlier in the year, the couple had changed their date from a Saturday to a Sunday and I had forgotten to update the booking calendar. Luckily, we don't book weddings on Sundays, so we just stayed another night.

This taught me a valuable lesson: always double-check, even triple-check, your information. Being prepared starts with having all the key information available and correct. In this letter, I'll go through my preparation process. Hopefully, it will give you some inspiration for how to prepare well for your next shoot. Trust me, you'll never regret being too prepared for a wedding.

Once the day begins, you'll be so busy focusing on capturing moments and engaging with people that it's easy to forget details. Information like a bride's cell phone number or the location where the groom is getting ready. You want these details recorded and accessible on the wedding day.

As a photographer, you'll have three nightmares. First, you come down sick on a wedding day. Second, your memory card corrupts before you have backed up the photos. Third, you double-book two weddings on the same day. Double booking weddings is the stuff of nightmares. After being in the industry for a while, you'll eventually get an SOS from a photographer who's made this mistake. Don't be that photographer. It's not good for your brand and certainly not good for your couples.

I've only ever double-booked once. Luckily, I realised a week after the booking was confirmed and the wedding was still a year away. To make up for it, I arranged another photographer for the couple and offered them a free engagement shoot. They ended up happy, and no harm was done. But it was definitely a wake-up call to get organised.

To ensure I don't double-book again, I use an online customer relationship manager (CRM). I put all my bookings through this service and it gives me an alert whenever I try to book a wedding on the same day as another. This is how I discovered my mistake and I sure was glad I had a CRM that day.

I also put all my contracts, invoices, and questionnaires through this software. It's super helpful having them all in one place. You don't need a CRM to be organised. You might prefer to use a big physical calendar on your wall or an online diary. It doesn't matter how you do it, just find a way that you can easily check to see you're not double-booking yourself.

Once a wedding is confirmed, I send the couple a short questionnaire. In this, they provide all the information they currently have about the wedding. Most of the time, there are several things that aren't completed, and that's fine, but this is a great time to get organised.

This questionnaire includes:

- wedding date; wedding day of the week,

- ceremony location, reception location,

- bride and groom's name, email, and cell phone number,

- information about what the couple likes about our photography style.

Six weeks out from the wedding, I send my couples another questionnaire. In this one, I check for any new information my clients didn't have when they booked. I also ask them for their contact details again in case anything has changed. It also includes confirmation of the wedding date and day — just in case — along with all the important locations, start times, and names of the bridal party members. This last one is really handy so that when I forget the name of a groomsman or bridesmaid, I've got it there in my pocket.

I also include information about family formal photos and send my couples a group photo template. I ask them to add or subtract any photos they're wanting. Having this list prepared well before the wedding day is an absolute lifesaver and will prevent a lot of wasted time or disappointment.

Family photos are some of the most dreaded and important pictures you'll take on a wedding day. They are also likely to be the most treasured and shared. These photos are ones that will grace mantelpieces, office desks, and be used when a family member passes away.

In capturing them, you'll face bossy aunties, lost brothers, and family members who don't want to be within 100m of each other. It can be a stressful time for everyone involved. The best way to get around this is to be prepared and have a plan for the wedding day.

The next part of wedding preparation is scouting out the location of the ceremony and reception. This is really important, particularly when you are starting out or haven't been to a location before. Even if you have visited a location before, it's a good idea to see it again. Preferably the week of the wedding as the light will change depending on the time of the year.

There might also be physical changes to the

location. I often photographed bridal parties in a pine forest near a popular wedding venue. It was great until I checked it out the day before a wedding and found the entire forest had been logged! Do your homework and find the spots you're wanting for bridal party photos. You'll have a lot more confidence as a photographer if you have some great photo locations ready to go. If you can't scout a wedding location, then use Google Earth or Maps to scope the places where you want to shoot.

Along with scouting locations, I try to see my couples the day before or call them. This goes a long way in building a connection and means you can go over the plan for the wedding. Often, I see my couples at their ceremony rehearsal. You don't need to be at the rehearsal once you've shot a few weddings, but it's a prearranged time you can make use of. Many couples will already be feeling stressed and won't want another meeting. It also shows you're totally engaged in their wedding. When you're starting out, I would recommend you stick around for the rehearsal. This will help you know when important moments happen. If you don't have time to attend the rehearsal, just call them.

It takes practise to form a habit of being organised for events that are usually planned over a year in advance. In that time, plenty of things can change in your own life, the life of the couple, or in the world. Being prepared will ensure you can be fully focused on your role as a photographer. You only get one chance to capture moments on a wedding day, so it pays to know all the important information — like the day of the week.

Your friend,

B.W.

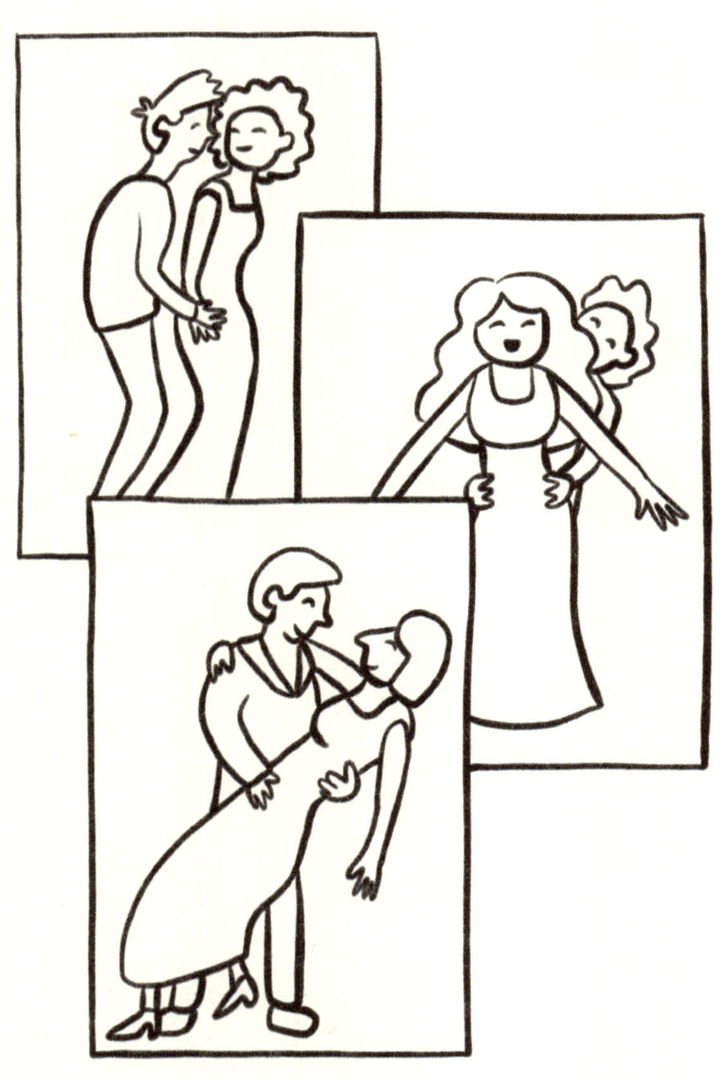

6 POSING COUPLES

I LOOK FOR THE UNGUARDED MOMENT, THE ESSENTIAL SOUL PEEKING OUT,

EXPERIENCE ETCHED ON A PERSON'S FACE

STEVE MCCURRY

Dear Charlie,

Thanks for sending me some of your recent wedding photos. You captured some beautiful images, I particularly liked the ones in the sand dunes. How did it feel when you were posing the couple? The placement of them was good, but the couple seemed a little stiff.

There's chemistry between a bride and groom, and it's your job as the photographer to bring this out. Posing is about the connection between our subjects. It's also about the connection between you and them.

A few years ago, Claudia and I were shooting a wedding in Golden Bay — one of our favourite places in New Zealand. They held the wedding on a private farm, with a hilltop ceremony overlooking the bay and the reception in a woolshed.

It was a dream wedding, and we finished it as we usually do, with a sunset photoshoot. During bridal shoots, I try to keep things relaxed so I include a lot of chatting, walking, and dancing. My recipe for posing is to find a good location with beautiful light and get the couple enjoying each other. This wedding was the perfect opportunity to use a tried-and-true formula.

At sunset, we took the couple up to the edge of a hilltop and had lots of fun taking beautiful, relaxed images. When the end of the night came, we said goodbye to the couple and their friends. The bride and groom thanked us for doing such a great job, saying that we were amazing photographers, even though they hadn't yet seen a single photo. What we had done was build a great connection with the couple.

Natural posing starts with a great connection. If you build a good connection with your couple and create an enjoyable experience for them, you're on the way to creating powerful images.

The way you make couples feel at a wedding will also impact how they perceive their photos. I've delivered photos from weddings that didn't go to plan, but the couples were thrilled with the images because they had a great experience.

The American poet, Maya Angelou, sums this experience up well:

"People will forget what you said, people will forget what you did, but people will never forget how you made them feel."

Great posing starts with the couple, so focus on them and make sure they are enjoying themselves. You can know the world's best poses, but if your couples aren't relaxed, the magic is gone.

In 90% of all my client meetings, couples mention that they aren't *posey* people or that they don't look good in photographs. But I believe every person looks good in a photograph — when they're relaxed and enjoying themselves.

I'm going to take you through some poses that I use at weddings to help get you started. It's helpful to have around ten options ready to go. You won't use them all at every wedding as poses work differently depending on the setting and the people. I'll walk you through five that I use to get you started, and then I'll send you off to find some of your own.

The Walk

Walking is a great way to both add movement to your photos and relax your couples into the shoot. I often use it at the start of a portrait session when couples are most tense. It's pretty simple — get them to hold hands and go for a walk together. While they're walking, get them to look at each other and have a chat.

To add a bit of fun, you can get them to bump each other's hips or have them run. Roads and paths are great places for this pose as you'll add some nice leading lines into the image.

The Crane Shot

The crane shot is a shot I use at most weddings as it gives a flattering perspective. Teenage girls worked this out years ago. People look flattering from a high perspective as you remove the possibility of double chins and general awkwardness.

It also creates a more interesting look that will add character to your photos. How you get it is simple. Have your couple cuddle each other and ask them to enjoy the moment together. I'll often ask the groom to kiss the bride on the cheek or whisper in her ear the most romantic thing he can think of.

Most grooms like having some fun or being given relaxed directions. I've had plenty of hilarious moments come from that suggestion and it's a great way to capture emotion in your photographs.

Once they're cuddling, walk up close, hold the camera above your head — or climb onto something — and grab some shots. Move around the couple to find the best angle.

Dancing

Getting your couple to dance together is another

great way to add movement into your photos and it helps them stay relaxed. Couples like to move or chat as it gives them something to do. Many couples don't have a lot of confidence in front of the camera and dancing helps loosen them up. Find a good spot with space to move. You can do this on hilltops, beaches, forests, jetties, and country roads — even parking lots.

On a wedding day, have them practise their first dance. It doesn't matter if it's just swaying in a circle. Dancing with a partner is naturally romantic and it will spark a connection between your couple. When you photograph dancing, it's always good to get a mix of close-ups and full-length photos.

Side by Side

This is a pretty simple photo that looks best when there are strong elements framing the couple. I often use this with architecture or when there are some trees to frame the couple. Once you've found a good location, the setup is simple. Get the couple standing side by side with a bit of space between them and have them hold hands. This looks best when it's shot formally.

You can vary it by getting the couple to look at the camera and then have them turn their heads to look at one another. It may seem stiff — and it is to some extent — but it's a formal photo that can look great in the right setting.

The 'Have a Cuddle'

This is the easiest pose to do but can be tricky to master because of its simplicity. Find a great location where there is good light and get your couple to have a cuddle. I tell my couples to give each other a hug or cuddle in the way they normally would. This gives them an opportunity to find a pose that works for them as they will go to their most natural posture.

The trick is in the tweaking and it takes some practise to get right. Once the couple are cuddling, have a look at how their bodies are placed. You want to make sure they aren't smothering each other.

Equally, you don't want them stiff and awkward. Often, guys will have one of their hands hanging loose, so either get them to put the free hand on the bride's waist, hold hands, or put their hand in their pocket.

You can foster intimacy in this pose by asking them a question. I usually ask them to "share your favourite thing about the other person" or "tell each other your favourite moment from today". This will relax them and evoke emotion — both great things in portraits.

I have a lot more poses I could share, but I want you to do a bit of work. Jump onto your favourite social media platform and search #weddingphotography or #engagementshoot. Have a look at the poses the photographers have used and find five that you like or want to try on your next shoot.

It's a great idea to use new poses with friends or with your practise couples. Take screenshots of the poses and make them into a list of shots you want to practise. The great thing about asking your friends to come and do a shoot with you is that they will expect to be helping you out.

This is a practise, so feel free to get your phone out to recreate a pose. Communicate with them so they know what's going on. Remember, they have chosen to help you practise new techniques.

Great posing starts with a strong connection between you and the couple you're photographing. Focus on them, ask questions, and get to know the people in front of your camera. A year after the wedding, your couples won't remember your cheesy questions or whether you needed to look at your phone for pose references, but they will remember the way you made them feel.

Your friend,

B.W.

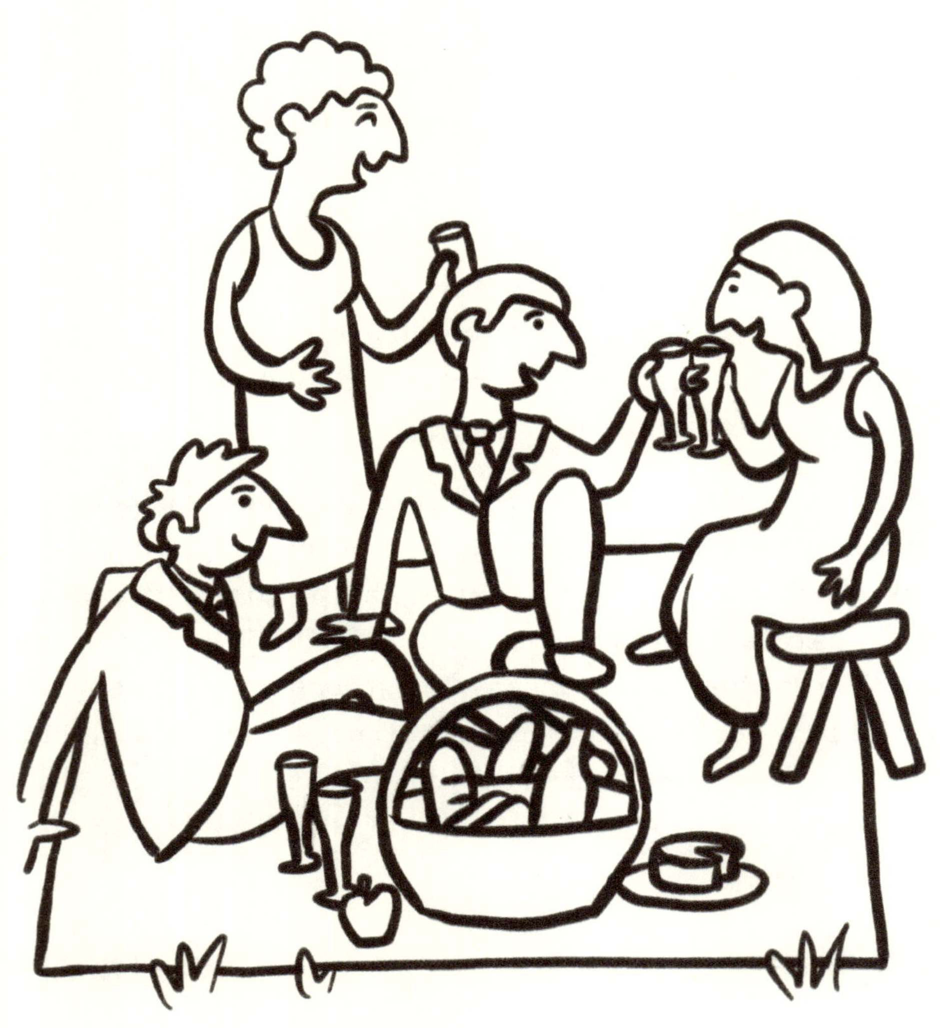

7 BRIDAL PARTIES

THE THING THAT'S IMPORTANT TO KNOW IS THAT YOU NEVER KNOW. YOU'RE

ALWAYS SORT OF FEELING YOUR WAY

DIANE ARBUS

Dear Charlie,

Working with people is a central part of wedding photography, and because of this there are going to be some challenging individuals to work with — particularly when there are open bars involved. Just like the guest you spoke about in your last letter — they sound like quite a character! Wedding days are a relational cocktail of romance, celebration, and family dynamics. They can be complicated gatherings.

The better you're able to work with different types of people, the more effective you'll be as a photographer. You're a charismatic person. Use your charm. Woo wedding guests. Be interested in them, particularly when they're in the bridal party.

Recently, I was photographing another wedding in

Golden Bay, and had just finished taking photos of the bridal party. The plan now was to ride quad-bikes down a beach to the reception. On paper, it sounds great. But, as I slipped off a motorbike, two regrets went through my mind. First, choosing to ride on the back of a four-wheeler driven by a groomsman who had drunk far too much Fire Whiskey. Second, my decision to hold on with one hand so I could take photos of the three other bikes, driven by equally intoxicated groomsmen — all of whom were carrying bridesmaids.

It's times like these that your life decisions come into question. Should I have chosen a career as a photographer? Why did I not take up that career at the bank? Is the job writing manuals for Ikea kitsets still online?

If you ask similar types of questions, then please know it is very normal. In taking up the vocation of a wedding photographer, you will quickly encounter the challenge of bridal parties. In saying this, many of the situations you'll face can be managed. You just need to follow a few simple steps.

The most important one is to connect with each member of the bridal party. If the bridesmaids and groomsmen actually like you, then your day is going to be a lot more enjoyable.

Whenever I start a wedding, I spend the first thirty minutes to an hour just getting to know the bridal party. I ask them about what they do with their time, where they're from, and how they know the bride or groom.

Building relationships early in the day always pays off when you do bridal party photos. The most important part of this is getting to know the names of each member of the group. Assume you will forget at least one name during the day. Always have a list of their names, either on your phone or written on a piece of paper.

Remembering someone's name will go a long way towards them liking you. Also, it's a lot easier to get a bridesmaid or groomsman to comply with a photo request when you ask them by name.

The second step is to feed them well. Things go downhill quickly once a bridal party gets hungry. I address this issue way back at the initial client meeting. When I talk about photo locations with the couple, I always encourage them to bring a picnic as it's great for two reasons. It keeps everyone happy, and it creates the opportunity for relaxed candid photos.

If you're not able to get the bride and groom to organise a picnic, have the bridal party bring a few drinks, along with some reception canapes.

You need to assume that bridal party members will think a photoshoot is going to be the worst part of a wedding day. Your job is to prove them wrong! You will have already set yourself up by getting to know them and keeping them well fed. The last step is to have some fun.

This can be done in several ways. Making jokes, going for a walk, or pulling some dance moves — whatever works for that particular bridal party. It might sound cheesy but it will relax everyone and they'll have a much better time on the shoot.

Keep a few 'dad' jokes in your back pocket when photographing bridal parties. Most of the time, people are feeling awkward anyway and are looking for opportunities to laugh.

These are a few I use, but you're a lot cooler than I am, so feel free to use your own material:

- Look at the person most likely to get hit on by a wedding guest.

- Show me your best dance move.

- Look at the person who's going to drink the most beer today.

- Think of your best pickup line and share it with the bridesmaid/groomsman next to you.

You want to create opportunities for capturing natural smiles, laughs, and interaction. Jokes and icebreakers relax people. The cheese is a means to an end.

Remember that when using jokes, it's important to

get a feel for what is appropriate for each bridal party. Some groups will use a lot of banter and make fun of each other. With these groups, you have free rein to make any joke you like and they'll love it. Other bridal parties will be more sensitive and need more light-hearted jokes. If you've done the groundwork of getting to know the bridesmaids and groomsmen, you'll have a good idea of what humour is appropriate.

Along with humour, it also helps to have a plan. This will make things run a lot smoother. I keep the following shots in mind when photographing bridal parties:

- All bridal party members together

- All bridesmaids together

- All groomsmen together

- Each bridesmaid with the bride

- Each groomsman with the groom

- Individual portraits of groom, bride, groomsmen, and bridesmaids

I also like to offer any partner/family photos for extra relational brownie points

In wedding photography, you'll face all sorts of tricky situations. You can reduce the risk of bridal party photos being one of these by building personal connections.

Remembering names, organising food, and making things fun are all important. When you've got these elements in place, you'll more than likely love those weddings with 12 bridesmaids and groomsmen.

These are some of the most important people in the lives of your couples. Capturing beautiful, fun, and meaningful photographs of them will mean a huge amount. Bridal parties can be a wild ride, but once you've got the basics mastered, you'll be fine.

Your friend,

B.W.

8 WEDDING DAYS

WHICH OF MY PHOTOGRAPHS IS MY FAVOURITE?

THE ONE I'M GOING TO TAKE TOMORROW

IMOGEN CUNNINGHAM

Dear Charlie,

Wedding days require a lot of energy to pull off — even when you start fresh. It sounds like you paid the price for having a big night before your recent wedding. Spending a whole day photographing with a hangover does not sound fun.

As a photographer, you could be on your feet for up to 12 hours, often get fed last, and people expect you to be fun all day — all while trying to capture beautiful images. It's demanding on your body, mind, and emotions, so look after yourself.

Six years ago, Claudia and I photographed a wedding in the Abel Tasman National Park. I woke up the next day with a splitting headache, sunburnt face, and a mouth dryer than my dad joke repertoire. The photography hangover had set in. If I had no memory of the weekend, I would have thought I'd been to a music festival. A lot of loud music, too much sun, and not enough water. Fortunately, I remembered the last two days.

The couple were young, good looking, and heaps of fun. They had planned a two-day party for their wedding and pulled it off in style, starting the day before their ceremony with an elaborate barbecue, complete with cocktails and local craft beer. It was going to be a great weekend.

The day of the wedding arrived like a scene from a bridal magazine. Cloudless sky, warm weather, and plenty of well dressed, good-looking people. It was the type of day all wedding photographers dream of capturing. A day you want to show off to all your future brides. I was excited about photographing this one.

The problem was that, in my excitement, I forgot to pack a bottle of water or any food. This didn't matter too much at the start, but as the day wore on, my body became more and more dehydrated. Claudia, being more sensible than me, remembered to drink lots of water. I pushed through and ignored the needs of my body. Which resulted in a massive wedding photography hangover. If you want to do this job for the long run, you need to learn to look after your body.

When photographing a wedding, make sure you bring enough food and water. Wedding days are long and there often isn't time to purchase food on the go. Sometimes you'll be photographing in remote locations where there isn't even the option to buy food. You need to be prepared because it's hard to do a full day's work without fuelling your body. I always pack the following items:

- Two drink bottles of water

- Lunch

- Snacks

- Sunscreen

- Paracetamol

- Pocket-knife

- First-aid kit (including tweezers and insect bite ointment)

- Spare shoes and a warm jacket

This kit is to help you look after yourself, but it's also there to help you look after your clients. Because you never know what will happen on a wedding day. As the photographer, you're likely to be the most experienced person when it comes to weddings. The bride, groom, and bridal party probably haven't been to as many weddings as you. When things go wrong, they'll turn to you for help. Be prepared to look after them.

One item I always bring with me is a Swiss Army pocket-knife, and it often turns out to be very useful. The most common use scenario is when the groomsmen are getting ready and can't find a bottle opener. In these situations, I simply reach into my pocket, pull out the Swiss Army knife, and pass it to them. The beer crisis is averted and you've just gained a whole lot of social credit.

I've had plenty of times where similar situations have happened. Bridesmaids who need paracetamol or bridal parties in need of sunscreen. Not to mention hangry couples who want a snack.

It pays to be prepared on a wedding day for a couple of reasons. First, you're far more likely to get great photos from a well looked after bridal party. If you can help when unexpected needs present themselves, you're going to reduce a lot of stress. Everyone is going to be happier.

Second, it's going to help you build a strong connection with people at the wedding, particularly the bride and groom.

As a photographer, if you look after yourself and your clients, you're going to have a lot more fun. I can also guarantee you'll get better photos. I don't know about you, but when I'm hungry, tired, or can't open a beer, I'm not at my best — and that's without the emotions of a wedding day!

The good news is, a lot of these frustrations can be avoided if you're prepared and have the right tools at hand. Drinking enough water, having snacks ready to go, or a bottle of sunscreen can completely change your comfort during a wedding — and the day after.

Your friend,

B.W.

PART 3

GROWING

A

BUSINESS

9 HOW TO GET WORK

I FELL IN LOVE WITH THE PROCESS OF TAKING PICTURES, WHILE WANDERING

AROUND FINDING THINGS

ALEC SOTH

Dear Charlie,

Well done on photographing your recent weddings. It's exciting to hear that you feel ready to become a professional photographer. Time to get to work, and your question of how to get more bookings is a very good one.

When you start out, new enquiries don't just land at your feet. You need to hunt them out. The best advice I can give you is to start asking.

In our early days, Claudia and I were having lunch at a friend's house. Someone mentioned that their friend was getting married and was struggling to find a photographer. I knew where they could find one. She told me the story of a young couple planning their wedding on a budget who couldn't afford a photographer they liked. At that point in my career, I would have photographed a wedding for $20 worth of petrol and a buffet dinner. I gave her my number and asked her to pass it on to her friends. We ended up booking the wedding, and it turned out to be one of our all-time favourites. We still stay in touch with the couple, all these years later.

Their ceremony was held at a country church under a big blue sky, with the reception held at the groom's family vineyard. They pulled off a very on-trend wedding — for the early 2010s — filled with bunting and vintage dinnerware.

We got paid a few hundred dollars and couldn't have been happier. We had a great time, made some awesome new friends, and captured some beautiful photos of the couple. There were many great things that came from this wedding, with the most impactful being gaining a lot more work.

From this wedding, I learnt a valuable lesson: work creates more work. The more weddings you photograph, the more work you will get. There are three main reasons for this. First, you're going to be increasing the size of your portfolio, which gives you more content to share online. Social media is a beast that is constantly hungry, and the more you feed it, the more chances you'll have of getting work. The vineyard wedding gave us lots of photographs worth sharing. We ended up with five weddings because of other couples seeing our images.

Second, every wedding you photograph is an opportunity to connect with more potential clients. If you do a good job and treat people well on a wedding day, you'll make connections with guests that can turn into more work.

When your couples and their friends have a wonderful experience with you, they become natural marketers for your brand. At this wedding, we met some amazing people. Including a number who would eventually ask us to photograph their own weddings.

This was a landmark wedding for our brand and established us within the local market. Facebook was still popular among young people and the work we shared on our page spread far and wide.

Finally, quantity creates quality. The more you practise your craft, the more you try and fail, the better your work will be. There is simply no getting around the fact that the more you do something, the better you will become. The better you get, the more people will want to book you. Remember the gap between taste and talent? The more work you create, the smaller this gap will become.

You might feel like finding spaces to practise or getting new work is a challenge. I've got a simple process that can help. A key part of being a wedding photographer is connecting with couples. So, a lot of the skills needed for photographing weddings can be developed through engagement and couple shoots.

Here's what you need to do. Grab your phone, computer, or a piece of paper and write a list of your friends in committed relationships, but not married. Extra points if they are engaged. It doesn't matter how old they are, but it's helpful to keep in mind that the average age for getting married is around thirty.

Once you've written the list, select a few couples who you think fit your style of photography. Get in touch with them. Share with them that you're wanting to develop your photography skills and invite them to join you on a free couple shoot for your portfolio.

This is a great way to gain experience and images for your social media. Your friends will hopefully get some nice photos out of it too — it's a win-win.

The only way you're going to get better at your craft is by practising it, so make some work and share it. Put yourself out there as a photographer. The more work you create, the more work you will get.

A year after the vineyard wedding, the sister of the bride got engaged and asked if we would like to photograph her wedding too. They were a young, cool couple who were planning a country festival wedding on a budget. We were still taking all the work we could get, regardless of how much we got paid. I definitely remember charging $600 this time.

It was a stunning day. They took festival vibes to another level with vintage blankets, picnics packed into old apple crates and an espresso coffee-cart, all accompanied by a country-folk band.

It still has to be one of my favourite weddings. I've got a few stories from that day I might share with you in another letter. The images we captured launched our brand and helped to cement a look that would lead to a lot more work.

We never would have got this wedding if we hadn't been hungry for work, putting ourselves out there, and offering our services. Even when the budget was low.

It wasn't about getting paid at that point; it was about the opportunity to create work, get experience, and build our brand. Work creates more work, so get out there. Be a camera assistant or second-shooter for as many photographers as you can, even if you do it for free; screw the haters who say that you shouldn't undercut other photographers on price; and, if you don't know where to start, just start asking.

Your friend,

B.W.

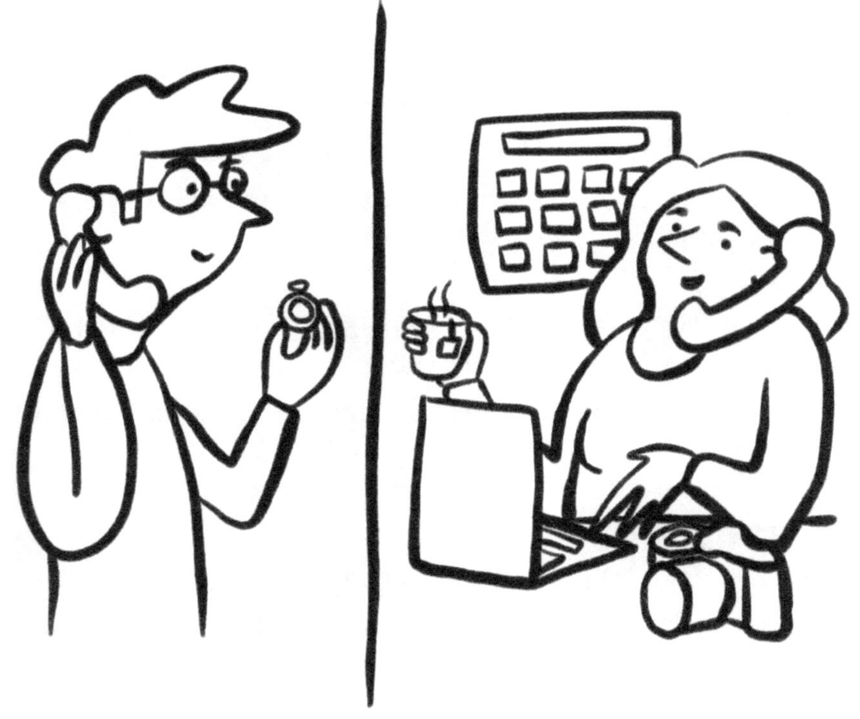

10 WORKING WITH CLIENTS

IF A PHOTOGRAPHER CARES ABOUT THE PEOPLE BEFORE THE LENS AND IS

COMPASSIONATE, MUCH IS GIVEN

EVE ARNOLD

Dear Charlie,

It can feel awkward putting yourself out there. I'm proud of you for stepping out and doing some free shoots with your friends. Once you've shared some of this work, you'll get more exposure. Which means you're going to have the opportunity to sell yourself and book more weddings. It won't happen instantly, so be patient. If you keep making work, then you'll find that bookings will happen.

When you get to this point, the next big challenge is working with your clients. Booking a wedding isn't just about having a nice portfolio or an engaging website. The biggest factor in booking is your ability to build a positive relationship with your couples.

Last year, I received an email from a couple who

were getting married in Cissy Bay, a stunningly beautiful location in the Marlborough Sounds — it was a dream wedding. Their plan was to gather an intimate group of family and friends and hold their ceremony overlooking the bay.

The couple had some great photo locations in mind. They loved my work and wanted to book right away, but I held them off and invited them out for a drink before they decided.

We caught up for a beer and spent most of the time chatting. We spoke about their work, how they met, and why Cissy Bay is important to them. I went over the details of my wedding package and answered questions, but it was a minor part of the conversation. It was a time of connection we wouldn't have had if they had booked straight away. Great images start with a great connection. Initial meetings like this are the perfect time to build strong relationships.

I knew they wanted to book me, but I encouraged them to have a chat privately before locking things in. I wanted them to be sure I was the right photographer for them. Being a wedding photographer is a great honour. You're invited to be an intimate part of one of the most special days of a person's life. This connection is important.

In fact, you usually end up spending more time with the bride and groom than any other person on their wedding day. This is why it's so important that there is chemistry between you and your clients. If there's not, you're in for a challenge. Not just on the wedding day, but before and after too!

Once I finished meeting with the couple, I felt we had made a strong connection and I was looking forward to hearing from them. Which happened within the hour, when the groom emailed me, wanting to confirm the booking. It doesn't always work out like this and there have been a few times where I've had a couple want to book and then decide not to after meeting me.

This can seem disappointing, but I was happy those couples didn't book. I wasn't the photographer for them. If they had booked, then we would have frustrated each other and no one would have had a good time. Remember, your job is to serve your couples. You want to do what's best for them, not the other way around.

It might be helpful to give you a rundown of how I work with clients. I've developed this process over my career and find that it works well for me. It helps my clients feel supported and connected from initial enquiry through to delivery of the photos.

My workflow starts when a client emails me inquiring about price and date availability. This is a great chance to make a first impression, so I will try to get back to them by the next weekday. I don't always hit this mark, but that's my target.

In this email, I greet them, get excited about

their wedding, answer questions, and invite them for a coffee. When I meet with couples, I always keep things focused on them. I want to know their story as a couple.

This isn't a sales technique. I genuinely want to get to know them. To build a connection so they can be sure I will be a good fit for their wedding.

I go through my wedding package and talk through my style with them, but this usually accounts for about 20% of our time together. The other 80% is chatting and getting to know one another.

Once a couple wants to book, I send them a contract that outlines what they can expect from me and what I expect from them. Contracts are important because they provide your couples with clear expectations. I also get them to fill out a short questionnaire. This outlines all the information about the wedding they currently have, such as names, dates, and contact information.

Finally, I send an invoice for the deposit. Deposits are important because it locks the booking in. It's a payment committing me to a date and a binding agreement that I won't take on any other commitments that day.

Six weeks before the wedding, I get back in touch with the couple and send them three things. First, is a final questionnaire which provides information on locations, timings, and names of the bridal party.

All this information is key because you don't want to be asking a stressed bride about wedding details the day before her wedding.

Second, I send a group photo template that has common photos couples want. This is important as family formal photos can be an absolute nightmare if you aren't organised.

Finally, I send a reminder about the balance of the booking to pay. I get my couples to pay the balance two weeks before the wedding, but you can make a timeline that works best for you.

It's not always possible to meet the couple again before their wedding, but when possible, I try to make space to meet at the ceremony rehearsal. Meeting before the rehearsal is great because it's a place to reconnect with the bride and groom and meet their bridal party. If you don't have time to do this, just give them a phone call.

You can take this opportunity to go over the plan for the wedding day and also do some location scouting. Having a good connection with your couple and a plan will mean you'll have a far better wedding photography experience.

Once I've met with the couple, recorded all the details, scouted the locations, and got a plan, the only thing left to do is photograph the wedding. This topic deserves its own letter, so we can talk about this more another time.

For delivery of photos, the best rule of thumb is to under-sell and over-deliver. You want to set the expectations in a way that you can be sure your couples will be stoked. I do this a couple of ways.

First, by setting the expectation that I will deliver photos six weeks after the wedding and aim to have them sent within four. This means that most of our weddings are delivered two weeks early, which clients love.

Second, I set the number of photos for a full wedding at around 600 but usually deliver 700-1000. This means that couples are getting a lot more, and it also gives flexibility to cull back if there aren't as many strong photos.

The last step of the entire process is a follow-up or check-in. A couple of weeks after delivering the photos, I'll email and ask if everything is OK. This is a great time to help with any troubleshooting or fix issues. If the couples are happy, then I also ask if they could do an online review for us. Most are willing and it's a great way to get feedback and increase web presence.

This has been a longer letter because working with clients is at the core of your photography business. There cannot be a business without clients. Learning how to work well with them will dramatically increase your chances of success.

I would encourage you to make a list of all the points of contact you will have with your couples. Create a plan for how you can make this contact a great experience for them and productive for your business. Feel free to use any of my headings, and add any others you can think of. Make a plan and be intentional with your clients. Remember, our job is to serve our couples. If you build great relationships with your clients, then you'll have no trouble booking weddings.

Your friend,

B.W.

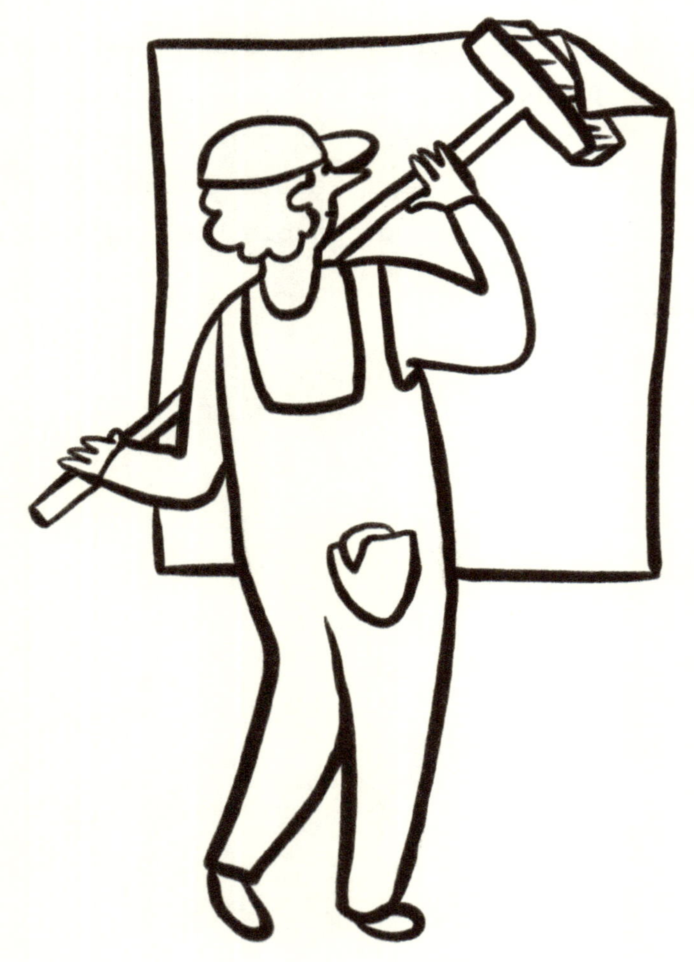

11 BUILDING A BRAND

IF I HAVE ANY 'MESSAGE' WORTH GIVING TO A BEGINNER, IT IS THAT THERE ARE

NO SHORTCUTS IN PHOTOGRAPHY

EDWARD WESTON

Dear Charlie,

Sometimes you just don't get the gig. I can feel that you're frustrated after a couple chose another photographer over you. This is one of the more challenging parts of starting out in a competitive industry.

Building a popular brand takes time, but you can fast-track the process. Creating work that showcases your unique voice and providing a positive client experience is at the heart of this.

A number of years ago, I photographed a country wedding in a barn outside of Nelson. The day was filled with outdoor games, homemade cider, and dancing. It had the distinct feel of an English country festival, which was very on-trend.

The couple, Kim and Gareth, loved it. Not only did they plan an amazing wedding, but also hand-built all the games and tables. They were incredibly creative in their wedding planning and loved doing it so much that they used it as motivation to start a hire business.

Their business specialised in rustic, fun, and festive wedding equipment. Their timing couldn't have been better. The demand for festival style weddings was about to explode and they quickly became one of the most in-demand hire companies in town. They eventually left their jobs to commit full-time to the growing business. I learnt two lessons from Kim and Gareth. First, your brand needs to be distinctive. Second, you are your brand.

The only barrier to starting a photography business is buying a camera. In fact, you could start one with your iPhone. This is wildly different from other industries. Being a lawyer requires a degree and passing the bar examination. Starting a cafe requires an espresso machine, refrigeration, and staff.

With photography, you can buy a camera, build a website, make a social media account, and call yourself a photographer — all in one day. This is great because it means you can get going quickly. It also means you have a lot of competition. This is where being distinctive comes in. You need to stand out from the crowd.

Being distinctive is all about the story. It's

about creating and telling a compelling narrative about your brand which resonates with people.

All brands have stories. Your name tells a story. The photos you choose to post on social media tell a story. The way you compose and create images tells a story. Even the price you charge tells a story.

The distinctive story of Kim and Gareth's business is: *If you want a fun, rustic, country-style wedding, then you need to hire our gear.* The distinctive story of The Woods Photography is: *We create documentary, romantic, and adventurous wedding images in a relaxed and fun way.*

You build a successful brand by leaning into who you are and what you're passionate about. What makes you distinctive? There's no one else with your mix of skills and experience. Pour those unique attributes into your brand.

Unless you're starting a large company, you can't get around this fact: you are your brand. This is particularly true when you're an artist.

This means when people book you for a wedding, they're not booking your business, they're booking you. So, you need your branding and style to reflect who you are. Not someone else, not another brand, it needs to reflect you.

If you were to ask my friends to define my character, they would say things like easy-going, creative, informal, and social. You can see the similarities between my brand and who I am. This has made me distinctive. What makes you unique?

When you're starting out, it takes some time to find out what makes you and your brand stand out, and that's OK. It took Claudia and I a couple of years to find out what we wanted our brand to be. Even now, it's still developing. That's because we're still developing as people and artists.

Your brand will develop over time, but you want to be intentional about this. Once you know what makes you distinctive, lean into it.

Emphasise the best parts of yourself. That means the pictures you post on social media need to reflect your brand. The way you create a website needs to reflect your brand. Your logo, name, and email signature need to reflect who you are.

This is important. The brand you present and the images you share will have a direct impact on the type of clients who book you. You'll receive more of the work you share.

If you share classically posed images, you're going to attract clients who like those images. If you share rustic, country wedding images, you're going to attract more of those weddings. If you share modern, editorial images, people who love that style will want you to capture their wedding.

This doesn't mean you want to only photograph one style of wedding or be snobbish because a couple doesn't fit your style. It means that you are intentional about the work you share.

The work you share reflects your brand and will attract couples who want you to create similar images at their wedding. As an artist, it's important to express who you are in your work and reflect that within your brand.

This, more than anything else, will create authenticity in your work. It will also make creating work a joy as it will be connected with who you are as a person.

To help you with this, I'm going to set you a task — it's like the first one I had you do, where you explored why you want to photograph weddings. Set a timer for two minutes and, in that time, choose five separate words that describe your character.

After you've written this, send the same question to five of your friends or family members who know you well. Have them send you back the answers. Write all the answers — including yours — on a single piece of paper and start finding the commonalities. See if there are any answers that are similar.

Once you've written them all out, choose five you think best represent what you want your photography brand to be. Use these as the foundation for building your brand identity.

You are unique. There is only one of you and there only ever will be one. Let your brand reflect your distinctiveness and stand out from the crowd. As an artist, you are your brand. So, be the best version of yourself, and the bookings will come in time.

Your friend,

B.W.

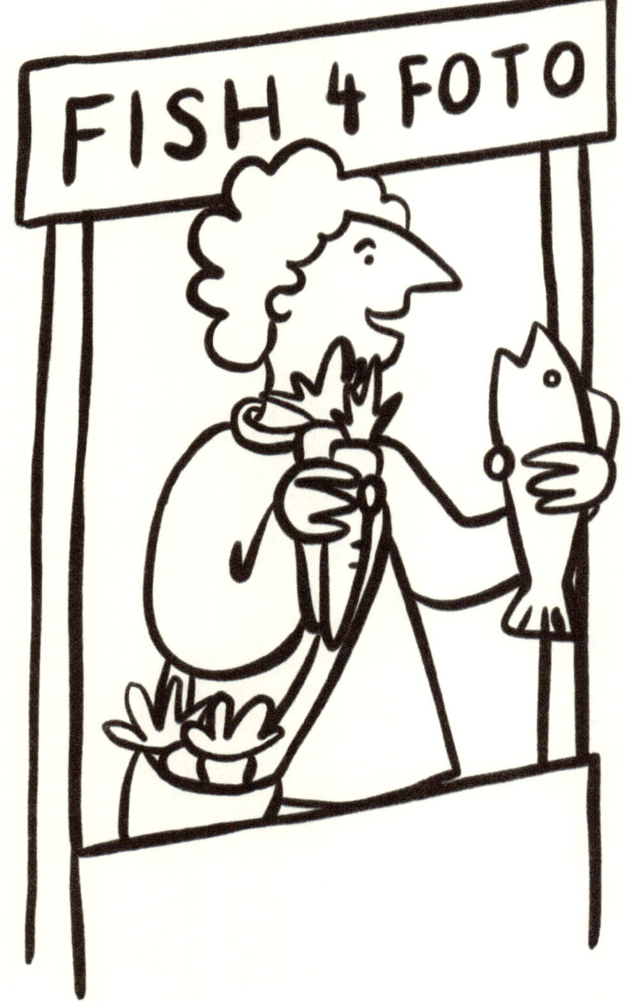
FISH 4 FOTO

12 PRICING & GENEROSITY

IN AN ECONOMY OF "HUSTLE", "SCALE", "GROWTH" AND OTHER SUCH TOXIC JUNK WE'RE #MANIFESTING LEFT RIGHT AND CENTRE, THE MOST RADICAL THING WE CAN DO IS CELEBRATE THE SMALL, CELEBRATE HUMAN CONNECTION, AND CELEBRATE MAKING THINGS AS PERSONAL AS POSSIBLE.

OLI SAMSON

Dear Charlie,

I get that it's been a hard few months. Covid lockdowns are a nightmare for extroverts like you and me. The first week is a pleasant change of pace — there are no social engagements, late nights at work, or jam-packed weekends. But by the time I reached the end of week two, I just wanted to see someone! There were plenty of struggles, but also a few surprises. An interesting quirk of the isolation for me was that it brought into focus what I valued most.

On the 13th of May 2020, New Zealand's lockdown restrictions were lifted. I didn't waste time before arranging friends to come for breakfast or inviting myself for a meal at KFC. Life was looking normal again, but there were several new things I learned from our government-mandated holiday at home.

When you take the time to stop for an extended period, what you consider important in life has a strange way of growing in its importance. For me, this was the importance of family.

Along with this was how valuable capturing memories through photographs was to me. Call me nostalgic or romantic, but there was more than one occasion during the lockdown period where I looked dewy-eyed at our family photo albums.

Lots of my lockdown habits faded, like the sourdough starter that died in my fridge. But the appreciation for family stayed, and it seemed there were many other people who shared this experience.

This is when a seed of an idea grew in my mind. There are thousands of families who have shared this lockdown experience. With very few of them ever having had professional photos taken. Why don't I create some portraits of families in front of the homes they had just spent an extended period of time isolating in?

Once the idea had taken root, I set to work, offering family portraits for free through our social media channels. I instantly had several families wanting to book me in for shoots. Over the next few months, a few times per week, I grabbed my Leica Q, jumped on a bike, and headed off.

Over the space of three months, I did thirty home portraits and captured some beautiful, simple memories. There wasn't any financial benefit in doing this. But there was a tremendous sense of satisfaction in giving something precious to those families.

Many of them had few photographs of the most important people in their lives. It was a great personal project that taught me generosity is a key part of the creative journey.

Being a photographer is a wonderful skill and profession. Once you're established and have the gear you need, the biggest cost you carry is time. Time and skill are both incredibly valuable, making them generous gifts.

Over my career, I've had the pleasure of being able to bless friends with photography as a wedding gift. Most of the time, they're grateful, but you need to be careful that your generosity doesn't get taken advantage of.

Part of the creative process is also learning when and how to say no. Saying no to clients who ask for more than you are willing to give. Saying no to offers of work where the only reward is exposure. Saying no to your friends who don't value the skill and time they want for free. Learn to say no.

It's perfectly normal and good to offer work for free or at a discount when you're starting out. It makes sense because you need the experience and your client is taking a chance on you.

Often, you haven't yet developed a professional skill set, but you shouldn't stay in this space for too long. If you continue offering cheap or free shoots, then you'll struggle to meet the costs of your profession, such as gear and travel expenses. You'll struggle to make a living from photography, and it will also damage your brand.

We live in a world where a low value is placed on digital products. We expect music or videos or photography to be free. But you and your time are valuable. The skill and service you offer your clients is valuable. The precious moments of time you capture are valuable. What you offer is worth paying for.

Pricing yourself can be one of the hardest parts of being in a creative industry. Early in our career, Claudia and I increased our prices for a full-day wedding from $1995 to $2995.

This was a terrifying act of faith, even though it was still cheaper than most other photographers. Racing around our minds were questions like: "Will we continue to get bookings?" or "Are we worth that much?". It turned out we got more bookings the following season than any we ever had before.

Humans have a strange way of perceiving price. If you put two chocolate bars side by side, one with a cost of $1, the other a cost of $4, we think the $4 bar is of more value. The price you charge for your photography will have a direct impact on how your clients perceive your value.

This doesn't mean you can charge $5,000 for your first wedding. You need to offer a service that lives up to the price people are paying. If no one is booking you, then check your pricing first.

Pricing is a key part of branding. Car brands are great for seeing this in action. Toyota and Lexus are both owned by the same company, and many of their cars are the same, except for cosmetic differences. Yet the prices between the two can vary wildly — the biggest difference is branding.

Toyota has a brand that tells the story of reliability at a reasonable price. Lexus tells the story of reliability and luxury. What does your price say about your brand?

I structure my pricing around the philosophy that anybody who wants high-quality photography should be able to afford it. Even if it's a financial stretch. With this in mind, I price myself a little lower than other photographers with a similar style. I did this because I want to be accessible, which is now a firm part of our 'why' as a business.

Before you go about choosing a pricing structure for your business, you'll first need to know how much you need to charge to break even. What is the minimum price of a wedding for you? Once you know this, you can charge anything you like.

Just make sure it fits with who you are and the story you're wanting to tell. It's a pretty simple process to understand your break-even point for a wedding.

You'll need to know a few things to do this calculation, including what your total yearly costs are. This would include things like software, gear purchases, insurance, and accounting fees. Then work out how much you want to pay yourself an hour. How much is your time worth?

You also need to know how many hours of work a wedding takes. This includes admin, client meetings, shooting a wedding, editing, and final delivery. Once you have those numbers, use the following equations:

Total yearly business costs / number of weddings = break-even point per wedding

Average hours of work per wedding x hourly rate = base wedding price

Is your base wedding price higher than your break-even point? Price your business any way you like, but it's important to know this number so you can be intentional. You may want to charge less for a number of reasons, but it's important to know that you're technically losing money.

At the end of the day, though, I want to be both generous and profitable. As photographers, we're invited into the most precious moments of people's lives. The work we do is art, and it should be a joy for us to create. It should be the joy of creating that drives us, not profit. Be generous in your work because there is power in the memories you are capturing.

Your friend,

B.W.

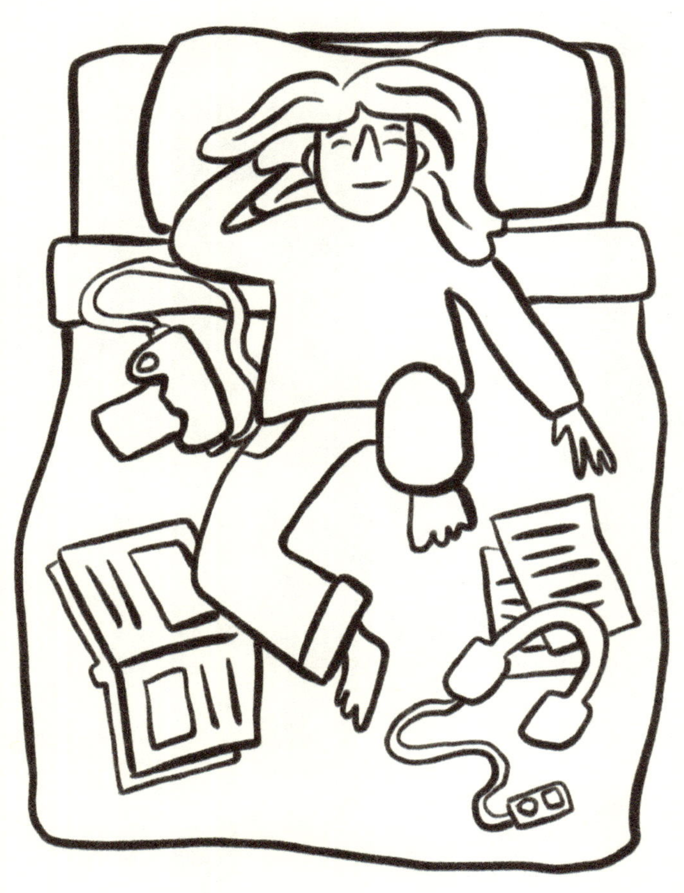

13 DON'T DO ALL THE WORK

A GOOD PHOTOGRAPH IS KNOWING WHERE TO STAND

ANSEL ADAMS

Dear Charlie,

At some point, you're going to need to face up to your tax return and full email inbox. I know that you'd rather be out making images than doing administration, but this is an unavoidable part of running your own business.

I want to encourage you that even though you can't avoid these tasks, you don't always need to be the one who does the work.

Right at the start of our career, I was sitting at Claudia's parents' dining room table in Greymouth, doing my tax return at 11pm. It was due in one hour. For the past two years, I had been filing all the accounts for our business and I thought it would be fine. I studied commerce at university and believed that I was more than capable of doing it myself.

Us Kiwis have a streak of pride within our culture that can cause us to not ask for help. Sometimes disguised as a do-it-yourself attitude. This aspect of my culture is great on a farm, 300km from the nearest city, when you need to fix a fence. It's not so helpful when you're trying to finish your tax return one hour before it's due.

So, there I was, trudging through the receipts from the past year: trying to work out the depreciation schedule for second-hand cameras. It was not an enjoyable experience.

I did eventually file the return and thank goodness it is now outside of the seven-year audit range! But, this experience taught me a valuable lesson — I don't need to do all the work.

Most creatives get into the wedding industry because they love photography or the freedom this work offers. They don't get into it to sit in front of a computer filing tax returns, editing photos, or spending hours replying to emails. But this is where many photographers end up for large amounts of time, particularly at the start of their career.

To some extent, you need to do everything when you start. Your budget is limited, but I want you to get in the habit of giving away as much of your workload as possible. You don't have to do all the work.

There's a mix of things that will make your life a lot easier as a photographer. Tasks that can be done by another person or sped up through software or a good workflow.

If you put some effort into setting up systems that ease your workload, you're going to free up time to focus on things that add value to your business. Things like photographing weddings and interacting with clients.

In saying this, you may love doing financial accounts or spending days in the editing cave, and that's fine. I want you to enjoy your work and one way to make that happen is through outsourcing and economising. Let's go through each of these and see if we can make your life a little easier.

Outsourcing

This is the process of contracting someone outside of your business to work on your behalf. This happens all the time in commerce. Traditionally, a company would outsource parts of their production to countries where land and labour costs are lower. The fashion industry is a classic — and not always ethical — example of this.

Very few large brands haven't outsourced a portion of their development or production process. This is because, when done well, it speeds things up, reduces costs, and can increase quality. The most significant type of outsourcing I do is my accounts and finances.

I get an accountant to do the work for me because they will take less time, do a better job, and free me up to do more weddings. It makes my life so much easier not having to worry about this part of the business. That's what outsourcing is all about — making your life easier.

I don't do too much outsourcing as I've scaled back my business to fit with family and lifestyle, but if you want to grow, this is a great way to do it.

I'll set you a task towards the end of this letter to help you find some elements of your business you might want to outsource.

Economise

Once you photograph more weddings, you'll find that your time is more valuable. You used to photograph one wedding a month in summer, now you're doing one or two a week. That's a lot of emailing, shooting, culling, and editing to do.

When you get to this point, you need to work out ways to economise your time by finding faster ways of doing a task. The easiest way to do this is through identifying repetitive tasks within your business. Then finding ways to not duplicate effort.

The most common tasks in my business are replying to emails, editing photos, and sending information to clients. I've developed ways to economise each of these and most of it comes down to having pre-set templates for everything.

For wedding photography, I have two email templates set up. One called 'Wedding Yes' and one called 'Wedding No'. As soon as an enquiry comes through, I'll check my diary and if I'm free on that date then I'll send them a customised version of the 'Wedding Yes' email.

This tells the couple basic package information and invites them to catch up with me either in person or video-chat. I also include a custom message about how excited I am about their wedding day. If I'm not free, I send them the 'Wedding No' template. This includes a friendly message and a list of other local photographers who I recommend.

It's not just enquiry emails I have templates for. I have them for contracts, questionnaires, follow-up conversations, photo delivery, and thank-you messages.

These save me a tonne of time and mean that I spend less minutes in my inbox. Just make sure to personalise the email templates. Clients want people, not robots, replying to them. If it's something you do repetitively, put some time into finding out how to economise it.

Next to admin, the biggest time-sucker in photography is culling and editing. This is a huge part of our work, and if it's done well, it will help to set your work apart in a crowded marketplace.

I'll say this now. If you hate culling and editing, outsource it. Get someone else to do it and fill up that time by shooting more weddings. I'm lucky that Claudia is an amazing editor and edits most of my shoots for me.

If there ever comes a day when she quits, I'm definitely hiring an editor. If you enjoy editing, or don't want to fork out the money to outsource, then your best bet is to economise.

Make your process as fast as possible — purchase culling software which speeds up selecting images; learn the shortcuts on your editing software, and purchase a good set of presets you can apply to your images.

To help you in this process, set yourself a timer for five minutes and write down everything related to wedding photography you don't enjoy doing. This list could include emails, editing, or family formal photos. Let your frustrations spill out onto the page.

Once you've done that, choose your top ten most disliked parts of this job. When you've got that list, have a good look through it and spend some time brainstorming whether you can outsource or economise any of these.

For some, you might not be able to change them right away. Work towards it over time. This is a process, not a magic pill. For others, you might be able to do something right away. If you get stuck, message me and I'll be more than happy to give some suggestions.

We live in the golden age of outsourcing and economising. You have access to professionals from all over the world who want to work for your business.

There are companies in Australia set up to cull and edit your wedding photos. You can hire a designer in the Netherlands to make your website. If you don't enjoy emailing clients, then hire a virtual personal assistant in America.

The biggest limitation to your business growing is yourself. So, focus on what you do best — the things that add value to your business — and outsource or economise the rest.

Recently, I asked fourteen professional photographers the question:

What do you wish you knew at the start of your career that you know now?

The majority said that they wished they knew more about business or that they had focused more on it at the beginning. It's easy at the beginning of this journey to forget we do more than just photograph weddings. You're in charge of customer service, accounts, marketing, finances, and web design.

Admin isn't the most glamorous part of wedding

photography. But getting your head around this stuff early will make your career far more fruitful. Remembering that you don't need to do all the work is one of the most important lessons you can learn — unless you like doing tax returns at 11pm.

Your friend,

B.W.

PART 4

DEVELOPING YOUR SKILLS

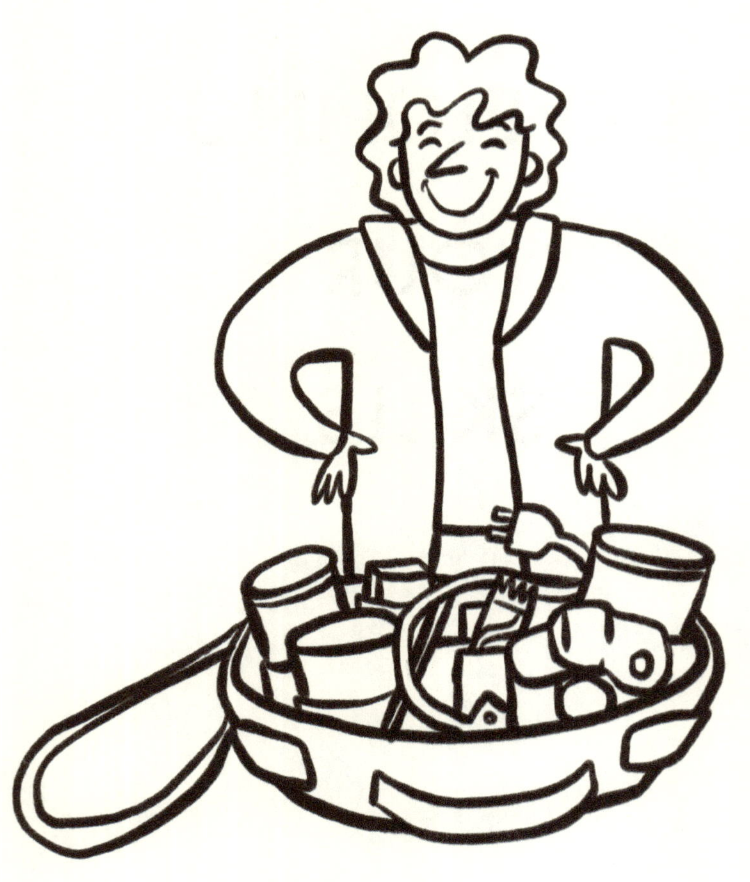

14 CAMERA GEAR

I HATE CAMERAS. THEY INTERFERE, THEY'RE ALWAYS IN THE WAY. I WISH I COULD

WORK WITH MY EYES ALONE

RICHARD AVEDON

Dear Charlie,

It always feels a bit like Christmas when you open a box with a brand-new piece of gear inside. One thing I love about being a photographer is getting to play with new equipment. It's exciting news about you getting a new camera, but remember, your talent is far more important than the gear you own. Let me take you back to 2014 — near the start of my career.

It was the hottest spring day I had ever experienced. The bridal party was getting ready in Christchurch, a one-hour drive from the ceremony location. Claudia and I had just turned up to capture the bride getting ready.

At this point in our career, we were building up our gear and had some pretty low-end cameras. The quality of the images they produced was a far cry from the photographs our current cameras produce, but they were all we could afford. So, here we were, photographing the bridal party with one very basic camera each on a hot spring day.

Everything was going well until my camera suddenly turned off. I thought it must have been the battery, so I grabbed one of our four spares. After putting it in, it still didn't turn on. I put another battery in, and it still didn't work.

Something had happened with my camera, and not only had it stopped working, but it was killing any battery put into it!

We were down to one camera and one spare battery, and it was time to leave for the ceremony. There wasn't time to get replacements, so we had to leave and hope for the best.

You can imagine what that hour drive felt like. We were literally praying for healing for my camera — the Lord was the only one who could help us now.

We arrived at the venue and made a plan for the ceremony. Claudia would use our one working camera to capture it, while I would pretend to photograph with my dead camera so it looked like I was doing something. Fake it till you make it, right?

We made it through the ceremony and thought we might just bluff our way through this one. Suddenly, our one working camera overheated and began to turn off every two minutes. This day was going from bad to worse. After the ceremony, I noticed a guest with a (at the time) high-end Nikon D800 camera. He was our only hope.

I went over to him, explained the situation, and asked if I could use his camera. Often, wedding photographers complain about *Uncle Bob* or wedding guests with fancy cameras. But at this wedding, Uncle Bob — who was a photography lecturer — saved the day. Our prayer had been answered!

Somehow, amid everything, we ended up taking the best photos of our budding career. We got through that wedding without it being a total disaster and we learnt several key lessons about photography gear.

The first thing being that you need a backup for all key items. Backup camera. Backup lens. Backup batteries. Backup memory cards.

For cameras, make sure you have two, even if this means borrowing or renting one for the day. You need two cameras. For lenses, make sure you have two you could photograph a whole wedding with. I mostly work with a 35mm lens on my primary camera and an 85mm on my secondary camera, but also have a 50mm as a backup. For me, 50mm is a focal length I could photograph anything with. I keep it in my bag in case a primary lens breaks or stops working.

With batteries, a good rule of thumb is to have double the number you think you will need. I usually use two batteries per camera on a wedding day, so I pack four batteries per camera. There have been a number of times where I've forgotten to charge one or two batteries. My forgetful brain is often redeemed through good planning.

For memory cards, I now only use cameras with two memory card slots. This creates two copies of every photo I take. That way, even in the rare situation that one card corrupts, I still have a backup ready to go.

Memory cards are inexpensive, so don't cheap out on them. Buy quality and be prepared to replace your cards every one to two years. I also don't format my primary memory cards until the edited photos have been delivered. This means quite a lot of cards, but it also means I will never delete photos before they are backed up in multiple places.

Finally, create a good workflow for backing up and archiving your photos. We have all our raw files backed up in physical locations and all our edited photos backed up physically and on the cloud.

Storage is cheap, and if a hard drive corrupts, it can be impossible to get those photos back. There are lots of good online videos breaking down a back-up workflow. Do some research, invest in some storage, and keep your photos safe.

We're living during the best time in history to be a photographer. Cameras have gotten so good that even cheaper models create incredible images with high dynamic range and clean high ISO. Many moderately priced cameras have features that pro models from five years ago didn't have.

When you're starting out, don't be seduced by the latest camera or by sexy lenses that cost four times the price of your first car.

What matters is you picking up a camera and making work. This is going to make far more of an impact than blowing your life savings on a shiny new camera with *pro* at the end of its name.

In 2020, I was attending a friend's wedding in Christchurch. It's quite rare for me to be a guest, but when I am, it's always fun to watch how other photographers work.

One of the first things I noticed at the wedding was that the photographer was using a recent base level Nikon camera and lens.

I must admit, my first reaction to seeing this was not positive. My little Leica Q I brought with me would have cost three times what her camera was worth.

She was capturing images of the most important day of my friends' lives with very basic gear! But I put that concern to one side. It wasn't my wedding and my friends had chosen her, not me.

Not long after that day, I saw the wedding photos, and she had created beautiful work. Sure, a pro camera and lens would have improved the sharpness and colour in the photos, but the moments she captured were beautiful, and my friends were thrilled.

Getting new cameras is a fun part of the work we do, but keep in mind that it's not about the gear. Our work is about capturing the moment. Spend your time developing yourself and your creative practice, it will be a far greater investment. But if you really need some new gear, I'd imagine that the best camera of 2014 is pretty cheap by now.

Your friend,

B.W.

15 EDITING & LEARNING TO SEE

YOU CAN HAVE WHAT YOU THINK IS THE BEST EQUIPMENT, BUT IT DOESN'T

HELP IF YOU CAN'T SEE

ANNIE LEIBOVITZ

Dear Charlie,

You're right, editing thousands of photos is tedious work. It's fine to go and capture a wedding, but then you have all those photos that need looking after. Images that need backing up, culling, editing, and exporting.

This is a part of our job that takes perseverance and skill. I can't help you with your perseverance — you'll need to develop that yourself — but I can help you with editing.

In 2008, Millennials started getting married, and they weren't happy. The prior ten years had seen the rise of digital cameras and social media. These changed the landscape of photography forever. But the style of wedding photography had been left unchanged.

It kept the formal, flash filled, highly-staged look adopted in the early 70s. This was no longer acceptable to twenty-five-year-olds. Brides and grooms demanded images that didn't make them look like their parents.

Existing professional photographers stubbornly refused to change their style. Out of this need, a new generation of photographers emerged. A generation that had the same taste as their clients.

Photographers who had been successfully established for over a decade started losing work to young image-makers — photographers who had often only photographed one or two weddings. It was an industry shift that no one could have expected. Taste had become more important than experience.

As this change worked its way through the industry, young creatives needed inspiration — because they certainly weren't getting much from existing wedding photographers. Many of them turned to the masters of photography and motion pictures. Composition, colour, and lighting in these works became reference points for creating images. There was one thing in common between these sources of inspiration: they were all shot on film.

The colour and look of film stocks from Kodak, Ilford, and Fujifilm were now reference points for how modern photos should be edited. This led to a boom in film-look digital editing tools and presets. The analogue film style gained speed and continued for the rest of the 2010s, fuelled by Instagram and high-profile creatives.

There are always going to be trends in the creative arts, fashions that rise and fall. It's important to recognise and reference these trends. It keeps you current. But I want you to develop an editing style that is your own.

To do this, I'm not going to share software tips or editing tutorials. You don't need to look far on the internet to find those. What I'm going to do is help you get started on the most useful process for editing photos — training your eye.

You have already trained your eye through the images, films, and art you admire. Through this process, you will have developed a taste for how a photo should look and be edited. This can be a great thing if you put in the work to develop your taste. It can also be terrible if you're not intentional about what you're consuming.

Be intentional about how you're training your eye. If you want your images to have rich tones, look at Sebastião Salgado's landscapes. If you want to tell stories with colour, see how Alex Webb paints narratives. To create images with character, be inspired by Sally Mann's photography of family life.

If you make a habit of being inspired by masters, you'll soon find that your own images will take on some of their attributes. Every great photographer wants to share the way they see the world with you, take up the opportunity.

Here's an exercise to help you develop this skill. Before your next photo editing session, choose a photographer you admire. It can be a famous master or a modern popular photographer. Find a book of their printed images or view their work digitally.

Remove any distractions and spend at least ten minutes looking through the images. Relax and allow yourself the time to soak in their work. Consider the way they have framed images, the choices of film stock, or digital technique. How much contrast is there in the images? Are the colour images saturated or muted? Are the black and white images warm or cool?

Once your eyes have adjusted to the images, switch over to editing your own photographs. Don't worry too much about trying to emulate the images you've been looking at, just edit as you normally would.

Once you've finished, look over the inspiration photographs once more. See if there are any elements you have added into your own images. Unless you really didn't like the photographs, I'm sure you will find some.

Choosing the perfect source of inspiration isn't the focus of this exercise. The focus is on learning to be intentional. What inspires you will differ from what inspires me, and that's OK. It's important to realise how the work that inspires us has a direct impact on how you edit.

As the 2010s ended, wedding photography changed again as members of Generation Z came of age and entered the industry. They brought with them a natural understanding of photography, social media, and digital tools. This generation is primed to disrupt wedding photography in unexpected ways. Just like Millennials did.

The difference is that their taste is influenced by photographers with large social media followings. It's where they get much of their inspiration from, and for good reason. Many popular modern photographers have a mix of talent, personality, and social media strategy — all of which combine to create a significant online impact.

These influential photographers may only have a few years' experience, but people don't pay too much attention to that anymore. Popular young photographers are an incredible example of what you can achieve with a strong sense of taste, along with the willingness to publicly share work and a hunger to grow.

Before social media, there were only a few pipelines for sharing your work. Many of them had significant barriers to entry, such as gallery expenses or knowing the right people.

It used to take years to build a well-known brand within the photography industry. Now it just takes talent, taste, and a knack for social media.

Photographers who are popular on social media are worth paying attention to. You can learn a lot from them, but you need to be careful not to have them as your sole source of inspiration.

If you are only inspired by photographers on a specific online platform, then it quickly becomes an echo chamber of taste. Everyone starts editing photos the same way.

I encourage you to innovate, and innovation only happens when you take all that you are and all that you're learning, and create something new. Broaden where your inspiration comes from. Get it from books, social media, galleries, and film. All these sources will start to impact your eye and how you edit.

Millennial and Generation Z photographers show how the art you're inspired by becomes the reference point for how you edit. If you're inspired by Henri Cartier-Bresson, you might start to enjoy grainy monochrome images. When you are inspired by the strong and dramatically lit work of Annie Leibovitz, that will impact how you light your photographs. If you love the images of your favourite social media influencer, then you might imitate their look.

Be inspired by photographers you respect. They all

have something important to teach you. Learn from their work and develop your own taste for editing photographs. Just go easy on the flash.

    Your friend,

    B.W.

16 LIGHT

LIGHT MAKES PHOTOGRAPHY. EMBRACE LIGHT. ADMIRE IT. LOVE IT. BUT ABOVE

ALL, KNOW LIGHT. KNOW IT FOR ALL YOU ARE WORTH, AND YOU WILL KNOW

THE KEY TO PHOTOGRAPHY

GEORGE EASTMAN

Dear Charlie,

A great joy in this job is that it gives you the opportunity to see amazing places. One of the best parts of photographing in unique locations is experiencing new types of light.

A few years ago, Claudia and I captured a wedding in Wanaka — a ski resort town at the bottom of Aotearoa New Zealand. The settlement is next to a lake and surrounded by a mountain range. It's a stunning location, and the weather on the wedding day was perfect — sunny with a hint of high cloud to soften the light.

As a wedding gift to each other, the bride and groom had booked a helicopter, with the plan to fly up to the top of a mountain in the middle of the lake for photographs. It's what wedding photographer dreams are made of. The pilot dropped us off at the pinnacle of the mountain sixty minutes before sunset, leaving us to enjoy the most incredible scene. Every minute, the light became more and more spectacular.

Golden light on top of a mountain is an impressive experience. I can still feel the sense of awe a moment like that creates.

Even though we were photographing in an amazing location, it wasn't the mountain or lake that made it so special. It was the light.

If we had landed two hours earlier, the light would have been harsh and unflattering. We would have been up a mountain, but the photos would have turned out completely different — light is everything.

As a photographer, the world is your canvas and light is the medium you paint with. If you want to be a great photographer, you'll need to learn about the different types of light and how best to use them. Let's go through some of the most common kinds of light you're going to encounter.

Golden Light

Golden light is the go-to light for photographers. It's romantic, exciting, and beautiful. Depending on the year and where you are in the world, you'll get golden light thirty minutes to one hour before sunset. This light is best for creating dramatic, dreamy images with your couples. You're onto a winner with this light, so always make a note of when sunset will be on a wedding day.

When your couples are planning their wedding day timeline, make space thirty minutes before the sun goes down to sneak out for some photos.

I hunt for two types of images in golden light. The first is to put the sun behind the couple, creating a rim of light around them. This gives a golden halo effect and your couples will love it. This looks even better when you have the light filtering through trees or peeking over a building. You can also try getting nice and close for more intimate feeling photographs.

The second type of image is to have your couple at an angle to the sun, which creates dramatic long shadows. This makes for a more edgy look and can work really well if you're taking a wide landscape image with your couples. Golden light is beautiful, but it is only one type of light you'll have to contend with. Light comes in many shapes, levels of intensity, and colours.

Cloudy Light

Cloudy light is a photographer's best friend. Clouds turn the sky into a huge diffuser, which means you can photograph anywhere and in any direction. This is great for taking cohesive photos without unflattering shadows on the face or squinty eyes. The flipside is that it also exposes boring compositions and poses. In saying this, if you get an overcast day for an outdoor wedding, say a prayer of thanks as it will make your life a lot easier. Particularly if the wedding is at a bright New Zealand beach.

Rainy Light

Rain is great for growing grass, not great for wedding photographs. Most couples dream of beautiful, sun-filled wedding days. So, rain can affect a wedding in several ways. First, you're going to work harder with your couple, as they might feel disappointed that their dream of sunshine on their wedding day won't happen. Second, it will force you to be creative as many of the photo locations you planned will no longer be suitable.

Light on rainy days — I'm talking full rain — is also a lot darker than you might think. You'll need to pump up your camera ISO or open your lens aperture to compensate. The colour tone on these days swings towards blue, which contrasts with warm indoor lighting. You'll need to watch your white balance when moving from indoor to outdoor or photographing near windows. Rainy days are hard work, so it's always good to have a wet weather backup plan. If you have a plan and some sheltered or indoor photo locations, you and your couple will have a much better day.

Green Light

Green light is the most deceiving of the light types we'll cover. When you walk through a forest or lush garden, your eyes capture all the beauty it offers. But when you take a photo, you're likely to be disgusted at the muddy, green, and dappled result. Forests are difficult to photograph people in because they make people look green. To explain this, we need a little science to help us understand.

Light is made up of different wavelengths, and each wavelength is a different colour. When light hits an object, some wavelengths are absorbed and some are reflected back. The wavelengths that are reflected back, our eyes register as colour.

Let's use the sky as an example. Every wavelength, other than blue, is absorbed. That is why our eyes perceive the sky as that colour. The atmosphere is bouncing blue light back into our eyeballs.

Why is this important? Because green isn't a flattering colour for people's skin. The only people who have green skin are sick, and that's not what brides want to be on their wedding day. When photographing in forests or shaded gardens, the light is going to be green. Light reflecting off leaves and foliage onto your couple will create a green cast on their skin.

I'm not saying to never photograph in forests or trees. Some of my favourite locations are in these spaces. But it is important to be intentional about where you choose to take photos. When I have a couple who love trees and green spaces, I find a space that has natural light that isn't bouncing off green objects.

I usually find these spaces at the edge of forests or an opening in the canopy so natural light can reach the couple.

Low Light

Unless you're photographing a summer wedding in Antarctica, at some point, you'll be photographing in low light. The most common low light space at a wedding is the reception, particularly the dance floor. For low-light situations, you have two options. You can push your camera ISO, aperture, and shutter speed to the limit or use artificial light such as a flash.

Most modern cameras are incredible. You can pump the ISO way up without too much negative impact on quality. The problem with this is even if your camera can see in the dark, the quality of light will be poor.

Remember light wavelengths? In low light settings, the light bouncing around the room will be a mix of brown, red, and yellow. This will create muddy-looking colour images. If you're only delivering black and white photos, then this is less of an issue. If you want to deliver photos in colour, then you're going to want to increase the light quality.

This is where artificial light comes in. By using a simple flash with a diffuser, you're going to increase your light quality substantially. Not only will you get better-looking skin tones, but you will also be able to reduce the strain on your camera. By lowering the ISO, you will increase the quality of your images.

Using flash has a bit of a bad reputation. But when used in the right setting, and in a non-obnoxious way, the use of artificial light will drastically increase the quality of your photos. If you've never used a flash before, I recommend picking up an inexpensive one and practising with it.

Bright Light

Bright, outdoor sunlight is the most difficult to photograph in. You'll encounter this type of light while photographing outdoor weddings or doing bridal party photos in the middle of the day.

This is a type of light you're going to need to get your head around quickly as it's very common and lasts a lot longer than golden hour. Often, couples won't have much of an idea about how light affects photographs. They just want their wedding to be on a beautiful, sunny day with visions of warm skin and cold drinks.

Another reason why I like to see couples the day before their wedding is that I have an opportunity to coach the bride and groom on where the most flattering light is going to be during their wedding. I scope out the ceremony, family formals, and bridal party photographs.

Bright sunlight isn't as scary once you've learned how best to paint with it. The easiest way is to look for two spaces on bright days — shaded locations and edges of the light.

Shade is important because you want your couples to be comfortable. If they're out in the hot sun, they're going to get sweaty and squinty. I'll often put them under trees or find shade created by an interesting building. Just make sure that the patch of shade is big enough and doesn't have dappled light — this will not make for flattering portraits.

Edges of light are where bright sunlight connects with dark shadow. These spaces create dramatic and contrasty images. It takes a bit of practise but when it works, it looks awesome. This is the light you can have fun and take risks with.

Morning Light

Morning light is energetic, bright, and gives the promise of warmth — like a freshly lit fire in a cold home. Unlike golden evening light that you can get reliably on clear days throughout the year, morning light is a gamble. One morning you wake up and it's incredible, with a red sky and shafts of golden light. The next day might have the same weather forecast, but the sunrise will come and go without any colour. I don't often get to use morning light on wedding days and it's harder to know whether the light will be any good. In saying that, I love shooting personal work in the morning — particularly in Autumn — because watching a beautiful sunrise is always worthwhile.

Blue Light

Blue light happens in twilight. The time of day when the sun dips below the horizon, but there is still light in the sky. This is a beautiful time to photograph couples. The colours in the sky can look incredibly vivid with strong gradients that move from black to yellow to red to blue. I love using this time to create strong silhouettes of couples or use shadows to add interesting elements. I use silhouettes and shadows in this light because it's going to be too dark to expose them well. The exception to this is if you're using artificial light or post-production tools to brighten up your couple.

These are the main types of light you will encounter as a wedding photographer. Each has its own look and needs to be treated differently if you want to capture beautiful imagery. It's important to practise in all of these conditions because the majority of a wedding day will not happen during a sunset. Find a type of light you don't like or avoid, and practise taking images. If you hate bright, middle-of-the-day light, then challenge yourself to do a shoot at 12pm. All light is beautiful and deserves its place on your palette. It just takes practise to know how to use it.

Your friend,

B.W.

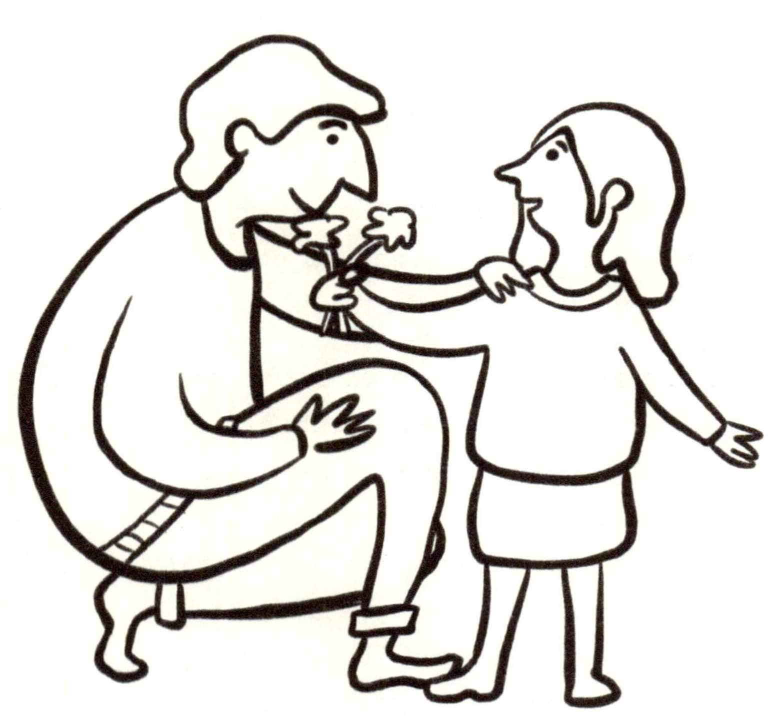

17 COMPARISON KILLS CREATIVITY

THE LIMITATIONS IN YOUR PHOTOGRAPHY ARE IN YOURSELF, FOR WHAT

WE SEE IS WHAT WE ARE.

ERNST HASS

Dear Charlie,

Unhealthy comparison does not equate to inspiration – it simply kills creativity. I was intrigued by the comments in your recent letter where you compared your most recent work to one of your heroes. You mentioned that you wished your pictures looked more like theirs. Inspiration gives creative energy, unhealthy comparison steals it.

When was the last time you felt encouraged after comparing your photographs against the work of another photographer? I would imagine the answer is *never*. Comparison is something all artists are tempted by. But it's not all bad. I want to help you find a healthy way to do this.

One winter, Claudia and I attended a weekend workshop

in Lake Tekapo — an alpine town in the middle of the South Island. It was being run by two of my favourite wedding photographers — Jake Thomas and Mike Hill. On our first morning, I looked outside at 6am and the ground was covered in a foot of fresh snow. There were ten other participants, but we were the only ones awake — along with Jake and Mike.

The four of us decided to chase the morning light. We jumped in my car and drove to the mountains — it turned out to be the most special part of our weekend. The day dawned with a pink and blue sky, set on a backdrop of the Southern Alps and rolling hills covered in snow. It was a photographer's fantasy. Add to this that I was hanging with two of my heroes.

Before breakfast, I photographed snow-covered grasslands, alpine lakes, and mountains, all lit by a soft sunrise. I enjoyed every moment. When I look back on that day, what made it special wasn't that I was capturing incredible images for social media. It wasn't that I finally created photographs which lived up to my own expectations. It was that I was able to be present and enjoy the process of creating.

At the time of attending this workshop, I had been photographing weddings for three years. I struggled to even call myself a 'professional' photographer. It was the early days of learning the art form and much of what I did was inspired by a select number of rock star photographers. Before every wedding, I would scroll through social media. I was looking for different poses or innovative shots I could imitate.

Afterwards, I would check social media to see if my photographs measured up. This was great for learning my craft, but not for my creative mindset. I was playing the game of comparison.

Every wedding shot would be compared to the work I admired. Did I do a better job than Mike? Why wasn't I able to capture that shot as well as Jake? Will I ever be good enough? Comparison in the creative industries is a deceptive temptation — a forbidden fruit.

We live in a world obsessed with comparison. Social media is saturated with highlight reels and curated feeds from hero photographers. If you're not careful, you can be sucked into a cycle of measuring your life and work against that of your friends and heroes. Unhealthy comparison steals the joy from the creative process.

When your mind is occupied with other people's images or creative works, it's difficult to be present with your own inspiration.

You have incredible ideas waiting to be made into reality. You'll struggle to make anything unique if the work of others is your only measurement. The art that inspires you should fuel your creativity. Not be a burden that diminishes the value of what you have made.

The only person worth comparing yourself to is your

past self.

The way you get better at something is to do it. To do it a lot. Every time you photograph a wedding, you will improve, though you might not notice it at the time. You might even feel disappointed sometimes when you don't live up to your own expectations. But over time, the little things you're learning will grow the talent within you.

The creative process isn't about one prizewinning image or capturing a dream wedding. It is about you and who you're becoming as an artist.

Let's explore an exercise in healthy comparison. Bring up the social media channel where you showcase your work. Scroll down to the very first picture you posted. Compare your most recent work with it. Is there a difference in style? Would you capture that first image differently if you could take it again?

Scroll up and find another early image. How does it make you feel looking at your old work? Are you a better photographer now than when you created it? If the answer is 'yes' then you are succeeding as an artist. This is what healthy comparison looks like — when you can look back and see that you've grown.

When I think of why I love the work of Jake and Mike, it's because their imagery is unique. They both have a distinct way of capturing weddings. Different from any other photographers.

There is something unique about their work, like every artist worth being inspired by. It will be impossible to create work that is distinctly Charlie's while you keep comparing your work to others.

It's important to have heroes, but don't limit your creativity by measuring your success against theirs. When it comes to comparison, the only question you should ask is: am I better than I was last week, last month, or last year?

If the answer to this question is 'yes' then you are succeeding. I want you to fall in love with the process of taking photographs.

If you make work out of a love of creating, you might find that one day you'll look back and realise you're now the hero. Not because you strove for glory or chased trends. But because you found your authentic voice by choosing to grow every day.

Your friend,

B.W.

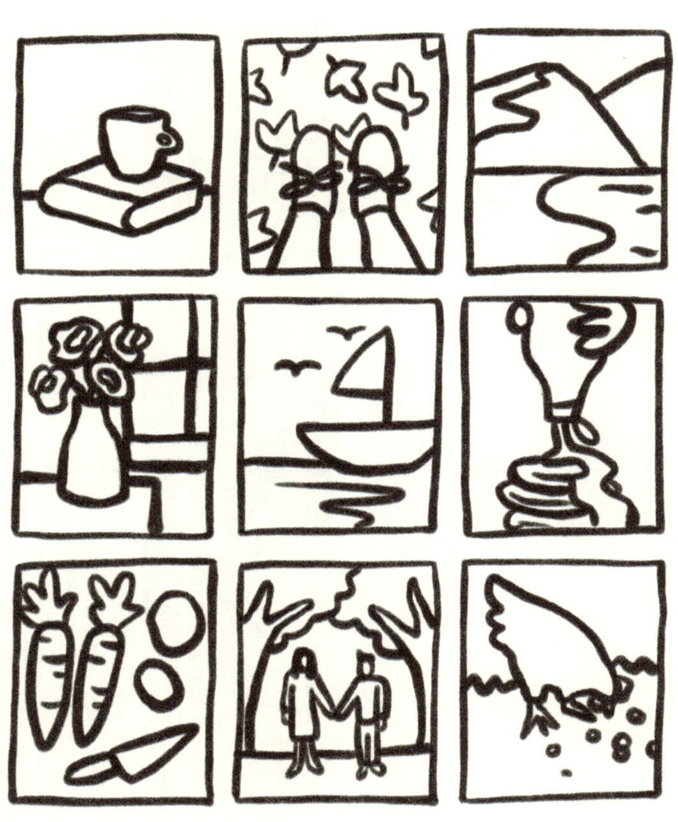

18 BE HUMBLE & KEEP LEARNING

YOU CAN FIND PICTURES ANYWHERE. IT'S SIMPLY A MATTER OF NOTICING

THINGS AND ORGANIZING THEM

ELLIOT ERWITT

Dear Charlie,

You mentioned your ideas had dried up. It's perfectly normal to have weeks, or months, where you're bored with creating. It's something all photographers face at one point or another, and is a great topic to explore.

There is no soil more fertile than your mind. But it still requires watering, weeding, and planting with the right seeds. To weed a mind requires removing unhelpful thinking, negative motives, or wrong perceptions. If these aren't dealt with, they will choke your dreams. The seeds we plant come from what inspires us — books, films, conversations, or the world around us. Finally, learning is the water that your garden needs if it is to flourish. You can never learn if you're not humble because it requires you to admit you don't know everything.

The only time you'll get bored with creating is when you stop being interested in learning. I want to encourage you to continue seeking after new tools. Be inspired by techniques you haven't yet learned and creative processes used by other artists. One common thing I see in photographers after they become professionals is that their desire to learn decreases.

This is understandable. As a person's workload increases, their time available for learning decreases. Try to be humble and strive to be a learner throughout your career — not just at the start. I am still working on this myself!

Soon after the Covid-19 pandemic shut down the entire world, a seed of an idea was planted in my mind. What would it look like to digitally capture the tools and stories of New Zealand's most respected leaders within my industry as an Anglican priest, then distribute them for free? Leaders and educators would record digital classes relating to their specialisation, with those classes divided into ten-minute videos. This way, high-quality training would be available regardless of lockdowns, health warnings, or financial resources.

As the idea germinated, I began writing a funding proposal. After data research, meetings, and hours of writing, the document was ready to submit. I had no idea whether the idea would land. Was it even worth pursuing?

Two months later, I received a reply. My application for funding was successful! This was such an exciting moment — until I realised my own limitations.

I was about to embark on a project which required recording twenty classes. Broken into 180 ten-minute videos with 1800 minutes of watchable content. The reality hit me like a 20kg bag of compost. I'm a photographer, not a videographer. How am I going to pull this off? It was only going to happen if I asked for a lot of help and was willing to learn.

I called up my friend, Josh, a professional cinematographer, and asked if he would meet me. Along with his business partner, Tim, he runs a high-end photo and video studio in Nelson. I pitched the idea of partnering together. Josh would act as an educator to help train me and my team.

I desperately needed to learn and, thankfully, he was willing to help. Without his input, me and my team would have struggled. This project required more than YouTube tutorials. Recognising my own limitations, and Josh's willingness to mentor me, saved the entire project.

I'm so impressed with your desire to learn and I'm humbled that you asked for my input. It's been a joy to write these letters to you and see you grow. As your workload increases, your time for learning will be squeezed. I want to encourage you to continue to prioritise learning. This will set you apart.

We live in the golden age of learning and advice. There are YouTube tutorials for anything you could ever need. Google is a great philosopher, willing to answer any question you have. There are tens of thousands of photography-related Facebook groups. Even with all these opportunities to learn, I want to warn you that some are more effective than others.

In my experience, learning via social media is great for specific questions. You might need help with a particular piece of gear or technique, and people are very willing to give their opinion. But if you want the garden of your mind to be well-tended and watered, then keep searching for mentors throughout your career.

Mentors can come in different shapes and sizes. They can be in your life for a moment or over years. Be older or younger than you. A good mentor is both an expert in the area you want to grow in and someone who is willing to spend time with you. It's the relationship you and I have.

There will come a time where our season together ends, and when it does, I would encourage you to find a new mentor. Someone with different skills and experience to me who you can learn from. Seek out a photographer and ask if you can help them at a wedding. Even if you just follow them around for a day, holding their bag. Watching how a photographer works is one of the best learning experiences you can have.

Don't be afraid to ask for help. Being humble is the beginning of learning. If you get rejected, try again. It's unlikely they were the right person, anyway. A mentor isn't only for photographers at the start of their career — they are essential throughout the creative journey. I've been a professional photographer since 2012 and I need mentors now more than ever! I am so thankful to my mentor, Josh, for his input and friendship.

Charlie, you've shared the seeds of many creative ideas with me. You just need to water them. If you want these ideas to become a reality, the best way to make it happen is to be humble and keep learning. It's also a lot easier to get rid of the weeds when you have some help.

Your friend,

B.W.

19 KEEP SHOOTING

TO ME, IT ALL IS PHOTOGRAPHY. YOU HAVE TO GO OUT AND EXPLORE THE

WORLD WITH A CAMERA

ALEX WEBB

Dear Charlie,

We all have habits that make up much of our lives.
Think of something you do every day — drink coffee,
have conversations, go to work, hit the gym, or scroll
social media. When you look into your past, you'll
find that it's these everyday habits that shape much
of your life.

When was the last time you took your camera with you
on a walk? As a photographer, it's important to keep
the joy of photography alive. The best way to do this
is by enjoying capturing the mundane moments of life.

There's a shelf in my room that is home to a worn
Bible, a tarnished jewellery box, and a beaten Leica Q
digital camera. All are well-loved items, used nearly
every single day.

The camera was purchased one year after my daughter, Trixie, was born. It might seem strange to purchase another camera when I already had professional equipment — but the tools I use for work don't inspire me like this little camera does. It was an investment into the memories of my young family.

Unlike wedding gear, I love carrying it with me wherever I go. It's small, well made, looks beautiful, and captures stunning images of the mundane and significant moments in my life.

One of the fastest ways to improve your craft is to take photos every day. There's no way around it. The more you shoot, the better you'll get. I've formed a habit of taking this little camera everywhere I go. It's contributed more to my skill as a photographer than any book or tutorial video.

The simple act of carrying a camera with you and intentionally shooting every day will transform your ability. It will train your eye to see significant moments in daily events. Through this process, you'll learn to visualise potential photographs before they happen — and be ready to capture them. This is a skill all wedding photographers should develop.

Last season, I was photographing a wedding in a country barn just outside of Nelson. It had been a sunny summer day, with guests dancing, laughing, and drinking. The groom had just sat down at the head table next to the bride and was opening a bottle of sparkling wine.

It's a fairly common event at a wedding, bottles of wine being opened. But I had a sense something was about to happen. I set my camera up, trained it onto the groom, and waited. He unwrapped the top, removed the protective wire cage, and began to open the bottle with his hand on the cork. I waited some more, then... Boom!

No sooner had the cork left the bottle a fountain of fermented grape juice spurted forth. The groom tried to put the cork back in, but it only made things worse. No longer able to explode vertically, the wine sprayed horizontally, soaking bride and groom, much to the delight of all the guests. It was a moment that happened in an instant and I was able to capture it.

Shooting every day trains you to see and be ready for moments like this. Make a goal to take a camera with you everywhere for seven days. Take photos of anything that inspires you. Learn to take delight in everyday moments and capture images of them. You're a talented photographer and the best subject is your own life and experiences.

Start taking a camera with you wherever you go, documenting the people and places you encounter. You don't need to share all your images on social media — you might even produce better work if you don't.

It seemed like a lifetime of memories worth

photographing happened in the first year of Trixie's life. If I didn't have a camera in my hands, special milestones would pass me by without being captured. I needed a camera that I could take with me throughout daily life, and my bulky professional DSLR just wasn't up to the task.

In the years since owning my Leica Q, I have taken tens of thousands of photos with it. I've captured holidays, everyday moments, time with my grandparents, the birth of our son, Ezekiel, and many more. They are moments that are precious to me, but they may be boring for you. And that's OK because my memories are my own.

Your memories and experiences have their own worth and value that I could never fully appreciate. That is the beauty of photography. Being a wedding photographer is a sacred task. It's your job to capture some of the most precious memories of a person's life. Every time you press the shutter button, you're storing a moment in time that a bride and groom can revisit whenever they like.

For a photographer, the things that happen at a wedding can become mundane. After a while, suits, dresses, ceremonies, family photos, dancing, and speeches can blend together. We see them week in and week out. But for your couples, their wedding is exciting, meaningful, and precious.

Learn to see beauty in the everyday and this will

help you to grow a deep appreciation for the couples
you capture. Your job is to faithfully and creatively
record their wedding. My encouragement for you is to
keep shooting — every day if possible — and to serve
your couples well. If you are diligent in doing both
tasks, you'll go a long way in your career.

Your friend,

B.W.

P.S.

I'll be in town next month! It's been such a long
time since we've seen each other. I'm looking forward
to having some conversations in person for a change.

20 THE FUTURE OF PHOTOGRAPHY

THE MOST IMPORTANT THING IS TO MAKE WORK THAT MATTERS, TO BRING

THINGS INTO THE WORLD THAT HAVE CONSEQUENCES

DAWOUD BEY

Dear Charlie,

Here we are, a few days out from me flying your way. It's been great writing to one another, but it doesn't compare to talking in person. Before we catch up, I want to share with you some thoughts on what the future of photography could look like.

Wedding photography can seem like a cheat code for life. It's a career with very few barriers to entry. The pay is good, and you travel to some amazing places — It's a career I love.

Since 2010, the industry has seen exponential growth. With demand for high-quality photographers increasing every year. It even got to the point in the 2010s where there was an entire market for destination weddings. High-end vendors would be flown to Iceland or

Santorini to capture couples with limitless budgets. The industry was a goldmine.

Then in early 2020, Covid-19 shut down the wedding industry faster than a jet crossing the Atlantic Ocean. In what seemed a ridiculously short period of time, every booking within six months was postponed. Couples wanted deposits returned and new work dried up.

After a decade of profits, the mine was closed, and it didn't look like it was going to open again soon. The global pandemic showed that even a seemingly fail-proof industry is not immune from unexpected events.

Starting in February 2020, one by one, my weddings were postponed, moved, or cancelled. During all this change, I realised I needed to reduce the volatility of relying on one source of income. Being a photography business and only shooting weddings was no longer a viable long-term option. Like almost every other industry in the world, I needed to diversify. So, I did something that I had done very little of up to this point — I started offering family photoshoots.

You'll probably laugh because it shouldn't have taken a global pandemic for me to realise this. Wedding photography had been so lucrative that I didn't want to do smaller shoots. They seemed like a lot of admin work for not much money, but desperate times call for smart business decisions.

After New Zealand's first lockdown ended in May

2020, I started photographing families. To get work, I employed an old photography technique — offering shoots for free. Using social media, I did several 'free shoot' competitions and built up both a brand and portfolio of images. Over the following four months, I did around twenty free family sessions. I used this work to build local awareness and a strong presence on Google – remember, work creates more work.

Over time, I got more inquiries. Soon, I had more coming in than I could book — which was great because I could pass referrals on to other local photographers.

This process taught me the value of adapting to unexpected changes. It also showed me the importance of not being too proud to offer cheaper services so I could build my brand and skill-set. During the Covid-19 pandemic, I saw lots of photographers struggle with the volatility of our industry, with many choosing to find new jobs or reverting back to previous careers. It broke my heart to see people giving up on their dreams because of something outside of their control. To thrive as a photographer in an uncertain future, you need to learn how to be adaptive.

One reason why wedding photographers were hit so hard by the pandemic is that weddings were their primary source of income. This was great while there were inquiries for new weddings coming in every month and their income was guaranteed a year in advance. But when things go wrong, there is nothing to fall back on.

If you want to create a business that is robust enough to last through the turbulence of life, you need to build multiple streams of income. The amazing thing about photography is that it is growing in demand and there are so many different niche markets you can tap into. You could develop commercial clients who need regular images for their online platforms. Maybe grow a reputation for quality real estate photos? You might love capturing new-born babies. There are so many options when it comes to photography work.

It doesn't have to be your primary focus, but offering more than one type of photographic service makes your business more resilient. It will also make you a better photographer.

The more photographs you take, the better you will become and the more demand there will be for your services. Remember the fight between talent and taste? The only way your talent can ever match your taste is if you put in the work to get better.

Since I started photographing families, I've found the skills I'm developing are transferring to my wedding photography. Family shoots might only be thirty minutes long, but they are action-packed. From the moment your clients arrive at the location, you have to be upbeat and engaging.

You only have a few moments to build a connection

and create space for natural, joy-filled interactions to happen. It's like a pressure cooker version of a wedding day. Everything speeds up. I don't know whether you have ever tried to take a photograph of a toddler in the middle of a tantrum, but it's rather difficult. Particularly when you're trying to create an image your clients are planning to give grandma for Christmas.

Family portraiture is all about being able to quickly build a strong connection, while staying aware of lighting, details and posing. These are all skills I've found useful on wedding days.

The future of photography is bright and demand for it will increase as the world continues to operate more in the global digital world. You're in a great industry — there will always be a place for artists who have taste and talent. I am also certain that the pace of change in the world is continuing to increase.

As we become more connected, trends, fashions, tools, and market volatility will be exported across the globe. This adds an element of uncertainty into our industry that we need to manage. I can't offer you a bulletproof solution to all the challenges you'll face in your career. But I can encourage you to develop your resilience, both in yourself and your business.

Many of the tools and skills we've discussed in our letters will help with this process. Sharing experiences with friends who can relate is always a good thing. Even better if it's someone who has gone through it before. The creative community is one that is generous and willing to offer support. Put effort into developing these relationships.

I would also encourage you to fall in love with taking photographs, whether personal or professional. Photography offers such a broad range of subjects because at its heart is the documentation of the human experience. Tie photography to the things you love or the subjects that fascinate you. Then, even if the world changes again and you're not able to make an income from it, your love for this art form will remain.

I feel blessed by our time together. I'm honoured by your invitation to speak into your growing career as there is a sacredness to passing on wisdom and experience.

My primary motivation has always been to help you in your ability as a wedding photographer. But I must admit, I have also used our time together to develop my own skills. It's only in teaching something that you can master it. My talent is still catching up to my taste. Our conversations have helped me to sharpen my practice and I want to thank you for all you have taught me. You have made me a better photographer through critiquing my own work.

I hope we can write again after my visit. I believe in you as a photographer and it's been an absolute pleasure to share what I can with you. Your skills have developed between each letter, growing like a well-tended garden — I'm proud of how far you've come.

See you soon,

B.W.

21 LETTER TO THE READER

MĀ TE TUAKANA KA TŌTIKA TE TEINA, MĀ TE TEINA KA TŌTIKA TE TUAKANA.

FROM THE OLDER SIBLING, THE YOUNGER IS CORRECTED, FROM THE YOUNGER
SIBLING, THE OLDER IS CORRECTED.

MĀORI WHAKATOUKI (PROVERB)

Kia ora my friend,

There is a beautiful concept within Te Ao Māori —
the Māori worldview — known as tuakana-teina. Tuakana
translates to *older sibling*, and teina to *younger
sibling*. This comes from the order within a whānau
(family), where an older sibling helps to guide and
instruct a younger sibling. If you've ever tried to
instruct a younger sibling, you'll know it can lead
to mixed results.

In Māori culture, this type of relationship can
also transcend the nuclear family into the extended
whānau. The concept of tuakana-teina is grounded in
the passing on of knowledge, wisdom, and skill to a
younger generation. This happens in many settings. It
can be seen in mentoring, teaching, workplaces, or
faith communities.

In Te Ao Māori, knowledge is tapu (holy). So, the passing on of knowledge is held as a sacred act. This makes the tuakana-teina relationship something of immense value.

My primary motivation for writing this book was to form a connection with you, the reader. The whakatouki (Māori proverb) at the start of this chapter speaks not just about a one-way passing of information between an expert and a student. It tells that both student and teacher have something of value to share with the other — both are partners of equal worth.

Through writing this book, you, as the reader, have taught me skills I never would have developed otherwise. You have taught me how to share and explain techniques that have become ingrained and intuitive. Because knowing a skill and knowing how to teach are two very different things.

Thank you for your part in this relationship. Both the tuakana and teina have something to teach the other. This is why I have written my book as a series of letters to represent a two-way relationship.

Letters between individuals are highly personal. They carry a sense of connection in a way that few other mediums do. I may not ever have the blessing to meet you in person. But through these letters, I hope you feel encouraged and equipped for the journey of becoming a wedding photographer.

In saying that, I would love for you to reach out to me via social media so I can cheer you on and hear the stories of how you're growing.

In the *Getting Inspired* chapter, I shared a list of my favourite photographers. I have books from each of these incredible men and women. I love being able to physically see the work of artists whom I admire. Having tangible art I can touch always inspires me. There are many photographers I look up to, but I chose to list ones whose work has a place on my shelf.

Through these books, I have formed a type of mentoring relationship with those artists. I will likely never meet them in person, but each has had a profound impact on my creative process and have grown me through sharing their work and words. I would encourage you to look up any names you don't know — you might find a new source of inspiration.

This book isn't meant to be an exhaustive list of all the tools needed for working in this industry. It's framed as a series of conversations rather than a textbook. When you meet with a friend for a coffee, there isn't a structured agenda to follow. The purpose of it isn't a business meeting, you want to be with your friend. The same is true for this book. I wrote it as if you and I had sat down for a beer or coffee, where you asked me a question about wedding photography on your mind at that moment. Connecting with friends is always best when it's natural.

Thank you for joining me on this journey as we have explored together the winding and ever-changing map within my mind, which led me to create the book you're holding. I'm looking forward to having more conversations with you in the near future.

Your friend,

B.W.

END

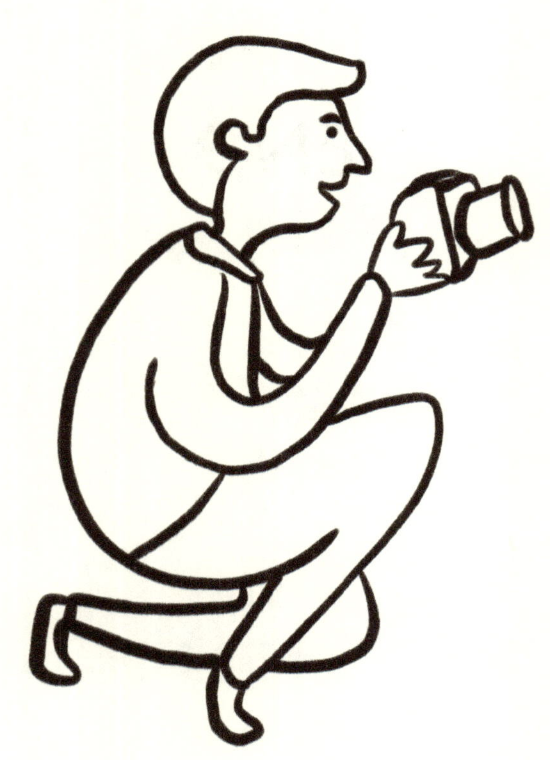

ABOUT THE AUTHOR

Brad Wood is a wedding and family photographer based in Whakatū Nelson, in Aotearoa New Zealand. He has been photographing weddings alongside his wife, Claudia, since 2012 under their brand, The Woods Photography. Brad and Claudia live in a little home near the beach with their two young children, Beatrix (Trixie) and Ezekiel (Zee). Alongside photography, Brad is also a priest in the Anglican Church of Aotearoa, specialising in youth work. He hopes, one day, to be a professional beer taster.

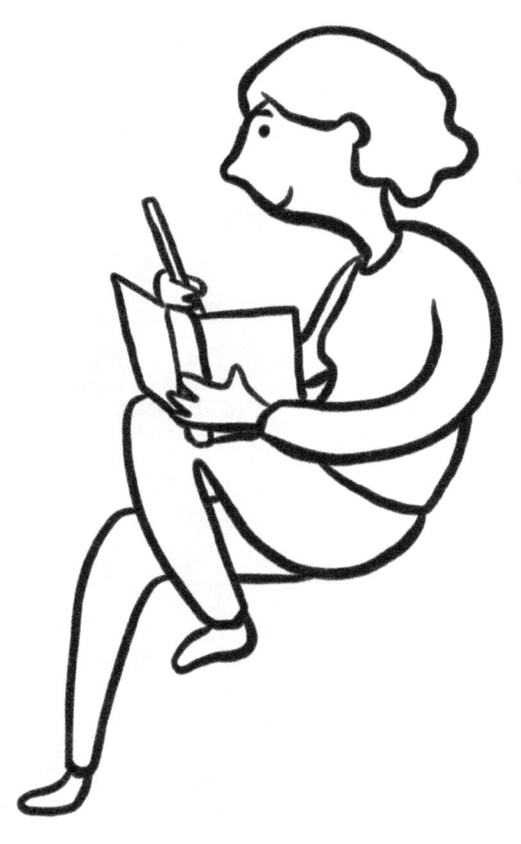

ABOUT THE ILLUSTRATOR

Petra Oomen lives in Whakatū with her husband Sam, cat Evie, and six chickens (yet to be named). She spends her time designing, illustrating, filming and photographing. Petra loves baked beans, the sound of rain, and brunch — with eggs supplied by her fluffy friends.

ACKNOWLEDGMENTS

Thank you to my wife, Claudia, for your love and companionship. I can't thank you enough for all the support you give to me and all of my crazy projects — I love you.

Stewart Nimmo, for your patience with me as I learnt a craft I knew nothing about. You are one of the most generous people I have the pleasure of knowing.

Jake Thomas, Ana Galloway, and Tim Williams for your input on the content. I have a huge amount of respect for your photographic skill and the kindness each of you bring to your relationships.

David List, you are intelligent, thoughtful, and humble. Your mentoring in helping me to learn the art of writing is a treasure to me.

Oli Samson, the modern photography sage who continues to inspire me daily. Thank you for the time and care you put into curating the community and educational content of A Strange Atlas.

My friends and fellow photographers from The Collective and A Strange Atlas for your input. A special thank you to Sarah McEvoy, Jason Renwick, Emma Wang, Ruth Gilmour, Louise Malcolm, Paul Benjamin, Nina Hamilton, Taylor Tudisco, Sally Johns, MJ King, and Dan Higginson.

Adrien Agy, good conversation and coffee is always plentiful when I'm around you — I am grateful for both!

Olivia Chamberlain and Charlotte Blythem, for gifting me your encouragements and eye for detail as beta-readers.

Kate Hampson, who generously gave her time to help someone from across the world, with her proofreading ninja skills.

Kelly Eden, my amazing editor. You have a gift with words and I am so grateful that you have shared it with me.

Petra Oomen, what a blessing it is to have your skills of illustration bring this book to life. Your talent inspires me every time I see your work.

Finally, thank you to Jesus — in you I am content.

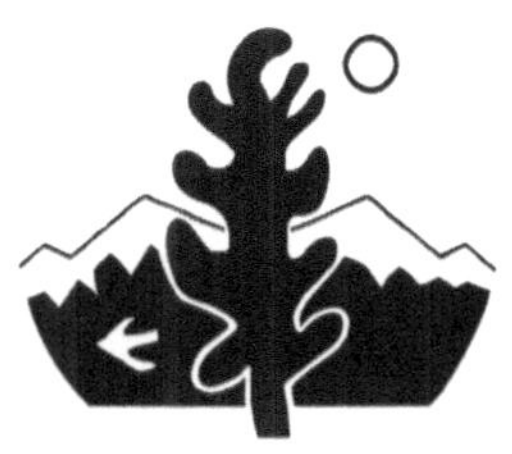